THE LIFE OF PYTHON

THE LIFE OF PYTHON

GEORGE PERRY

PAVILION

for Matthew

First published in Great Britain in 1994 by
PAVILION BOOKS LIMITED
26 Upper Ground, London SE1 9PD

Designed by Bridgewater Books
Peter Bridgewater/Chris Dymond

A CIP catalogue record for this book
is available from the British Library.

ISBN 1 85793 4415

Printed and bound in Spain by Artes Graphicas Toledo S.A.
D.L. TO-703-1994

2 4 6 8 10 9 7 5 3 1

This book may be ordered by post direct from the publisher.
Please contact the Marketing Department.
But try your bookshop first.

CONTENTS

INTRODUCTION

Consider this. The human species is up on the rest of the animal kingdom in being overtly possessed of a sense of humour. I suspect that our Siamese cat may have one but he cannot laugh, the effective way to communicate it, so it is hard to know. The capacity for laughter is one of the characteristics that separates out human beings from other living creatures; surely it has to be one of the distinguishing features of superior intelligence. Laughter serves an essential therapeutic purpose. Adversity is made bearable with humour – gruesome as it may be, men on the gallows have been known to ease their extreme situation with witty remarks to the executioner. Laughter is the safety valve, a means by which the hard life is made bearable, heavy-handedness is ridiculed, pomposity is punctured. Through humour even essential truths can surface. George Harrison, the ex-Beatle told me when I talked to him about *Monty Python* that 'Laughter is the great release.' It could not be put more accurately.

The British pride themselves on their sense of humour, even displaying smugness when foreigners fail to understand it. If they cannot comprehend then it is their loss. Yet in Europe it is the British who are more likely to be the butt of the jokes, just as the British make fun of the Irish whose humorous instinct is among the most sublime on earth.

But British humour. There was, getting on for four decades ago, a watershed in the evolution of British comedy. The press, called it 'the satire movement', a blanket term that could embrace such opposites as Harold Pinter and Ken Dodd. Certainly it was a good time for humour, and it all had much to do with social changes occurring then. The crucial event was Suez, in the autumn of 1956. What happened was a classic revelation in the emperor-has-no-clothes sense. The British Establishment, adhering to its traditional position without really knowing why, made a colossal fool of itself and demonstrated to the entire world, particularly important allies such as the United States and France, that it had no more idea of the realities of world politics than the humblest parish pump council. Unthinkable. Fallibility may have been suspected before, but never demonstrated on such a scale.

The ancient universities of Oxford and Cambridge were great places at which to be present then. It was the beginning of the long period of questioning and mistrust that would culminate in the worldwide young persons' turmoil of 1968, and in Britain was the engine of the explosion of creativity and assertiveness that produced the 'Swinging Sixties'. It was as though after all the years of deference and respect paid to authority, intact still because so many undergraduates had undergone national service and were thus subtly inducted into attitudes of Establishment power after passing the WOSBs, it was no longer necessary. You did not have to be a communist or a member of the hard left to ask questions. Even the Tories had their Bow Group gingering up and shaking ossified attitudes. With the abolition of conscription, which had affected thirty years of the nation's youth, a new simon-pure breed, unbought and untainted, was to hand. The Monty Python lot all fitted into that category, being just young enough to miss national service by a year or two, but close enough to have contemporaries who had been through that mill.

Nowadays, a quarter of a century after *Monty Python's Flying Circus* was on the air, it is extraordinary to find so many people still have a position on it. Scarcely any new young comedian can be interviewed on the radio without referring to *Python*, either by acknowledging its influence or, as is more likely these days, declaring a reaction against it to be rigorously pursued. Which is, of course, another way of acknowledging an influence. *Python* remains a strong force in British comedy. Repeats, films, videos, recollections all help, but the main reason is that although the members of the group developed as individuals, focusing their talents in many different directions, they were never embarrassed by the *Python* connection, and carry on maintaining their interest in the group.

That they are a bunch of university wits from toffee-nosed Oxbridge has sometimes been hurled against them at the hint of anything that can be construed as elitism. Of course they are thoroughly elitist. It should also be made clear that they reached Oxford and Cambridge by their own considerable efforts, and happened to be of above average brightness at their respective schools. Consider those schools for a moment. John was at Clifton College, Michael at Shrewsbury, both of which are distinguished public schools, but not quite Eton or Westminster. Terry Jones was at Guildford Royal Grammar School, Eric at the Royal School, Wolverhampton, Graham at Melton Mowbray Grammar School, Terry Gilliam at Birmingham High School in California. Their backgrounds were not deprived, but not privileged, either, representing in the main the sort of lower middle-class terrain that comprises that chunk of the population that serves as the motor of society. Michael recalls the huge sacrifices his father made to send him to Shrewsbury. John won a scholarship to Clifton and knocked twenty per cent off his father's bill. Eric was an orphan and spent twelve years at one establishment.

Cambridge in the late 1950s and early 1960s enjoyed a golden age. I say that unreservedly because I was there. The Pythons, divided down the middle between the two ancient British universities (Terry Gilliam, at Occidental College in California, is an honorary member of the Oxford side) bring out the differences in psychological outlook that prevail between the two places, which to the ordinary onlooker seem astonishingly alike, except that Oxford has a worse traffic problem. But Oxford, whimsically known as the home of lost causes, has a romantic vision. It nurtures concerned idealists, people who are prepared to put back-breaking effort into the things that they care about. Cambridge produces hard-nosed pragmatists, who tend to be rather good at certain things, get on with them, not wasting too much time on irrelevances.

In the Cambridge I knew it manifested itself in the utterly ruthless way certain people used the university as a springboard to spectacular careers. Those who had recently been there, like Peter Hall, Frederic Raphael, Leslie Bricusse, Nicholas Tomalin, Mark Boxer were already successful in theatre production, publishing, songwriting, journalism, cartooning and editing, as well as having become celebrities. Trevor Nunn leapt out in pursuit of Hall, Michael Frayn went straight on to the *Guardian* and then to the *Observer*. Bamber Gascoigne had his own revue running in the West End while still a Magdalene undergraduate. Peter Cook drew much of his undergraduate income from the West End stage. David Frost knew everybody at Cambridge, and was already mapping out a glittering career, fronting a dire series on the Twist for Rediffusion almost before his Tripos results

were out. The ADC was plugged directly into Shaftesbury Avenue, *Varsity* into Fleet Street, the Footlights into the studios of the BBC and ITV, and the Union Society, where names such as Lamont, Clarke, Howard, Fowler, Brittan held office, nursed the future government. To this professionally motivated Cambridge came John Cleese, Graham Chapman and Eric Idle. But for the allure of the Footlights and the Cambridge connection they might have joined the ranks of lawyers, doctors, academics and admen. Was there, and is there, a Cambridge mafia? Absolutely. But the point has to be made that those who use it to advance themselves must have talent as well.

Much the same phenomenon has occurred at Oxford during its long existence. The rival universities have bobbed up and down in relation to each other for centuries, so close as to make little difference as to who is top at any time. Terry Jones, impressive on the Oxford stage as an undergraduate believes that had he taken up a place at Cambridge he would never have gone near the Footlights, and would now be contemplating retirement in the next ten years from some exceptionally boring career. He and Michael Palin confronted the shortcomings that existed then in Oxford theatre and surmounted them by hard work and doggedness, whereas at 'the other place' they might have found the ride too easy. The two universities made *Monty Python* work, the differences supplying the ingredients that created the team's remarkable and unprecedented synergy.

With whom can they be compared? Not the Marx Brothers. Not the Crazy Gang. They were vaudevillians, born in trunks, raised in the smell of greasepaint, a million miles from the spires of academe. But the Pythons descended from their ivory towers to make the whole country laugh, without ever patronizing or talking down to their audience. As Philip Purser put it, when he was the television critic of the *Sunday Telegraph*, speaking of one of their shows: 'What other popular entertainment in the world could have wrapped together in disrepute Edward VII, Wilde, Whistler, Shaw, Richard Attenborough, Pasolini, electrical goods, wife-swapping, the cloth and, oh yes, *Come Dancing*?'

The Pythons for all their joint achievements have had singular successes on their own. Their talents would have been the same even if there had been no *Monty Python* although, in the cruel reality of things, capability is worth nothing without the chance to fulfil it, and the prominence granted them by *Python* was the trigger. With the exception of Graham, prematurely deceased, they are, in their fifties, able to enjoy the public esteem that comes to those who have had distinguished careers, and are approaching the time when gongs will be handed out. Heaven knows, they deserve them, if only for services to British exports. What is ironic, increasingly with the passage of time, but also predictable many years ago, is that they are now undoubtedly a British institution, and have become part of the fabric of that monumental edifice they had such fun trying to demolish.

GEORGE PERRY
London, July 1994

ACKNOWLEDGEMENTS

Books happen because many people co-operate with one another. Often the author is just one of a whole group of people who pitch in, and that was the case here. Gratitude is due therefore, firstly, to the Pythons themselves. They have over the years all been exceedingly generous to me with their time, they have lent material, shared their enthusiasms and told quite a few jokes. Much of what they are saying was first said in 1983. Sadly, Graham Chapman died in 1989, but he and the other members of the group, John Cleese, Terry Gilliam, Eric Idle, Terry Jones and Michael Palin, made sure that it was a pleasure to work on this book. I am grateful also to Charles Alverson, Humphrey Barclay, Lucy Douch, John Goldstone, George Harrison, Robert Hewison, Neil Innes, Kim 'Howard' Johnson, Iain Johnstone, Nancy Lewis, Peter Noble, John Tomiczek, Barry Took and Peter Thompson, and to Anne James and Roger Saunders in the Python London office. The picture research was carried out with smooth efficiency by my wife, Frances Murray-Scott, who also helped on several portions of the manuscript. Our seventeen-year-old, Matthew, a dedicated Pythomaniac, interceded with advice that was impossible to ignore. The genesis of a book begins with the publisher, in this case Colin Webb, whose flair as the head of Pavilion Books has made it one of the success stories of British publishing. High praise is due to Emma Lawson, whose talents as an editor are impressive, and whose calmness in the face of a daunting schedule was always calming and reassuring. Tim Clark enabled the production of the book to progress smoothly. Peter Bridgewater and his team produced an elegant and polished design in rapid time, and my agent Pat White of Rogers, Coleridge and White Ltd. gave me support and encouragement at every stage. In fairness, I should at this point mention our Siamese cat, Shorty, who throughout the toils kept us laughing, just like Python.

BIRTH

BORN 5TH OCTOBER 1969

LONDON

ENGLAND

BIRTH

The day it happened was 5 October 1969; the debut of *Monty Python's Flying Circus* on British television, the channel, BBC1. It was the first time that the public, primed by the reference to the programme with the funny title in the *Radio Times*, were made aware of the mewling infant.

Monty Python is a creation of the sixties, but only just. Nevertheless, along with miniskirts, flower power, the Beatles, LSD, *Playboy* Bunnies, *Hair* and the Age of Aquarius, *Barbarella*, the Kray twins, 8-track Stereo, bra-burning, and sundry other phenomena, *Monty Python* sprang from that era.

In truth, the antecedents of *Monty Python* stretch back long before that, to the immediate post-war period when the six constituent members were in their respective childhoods. The Pythons sprang from an age of vintage radio comedy, when television had barely begun its progress towards world domination. In the Britain of 1950 humour was derived from three main sources – print, film and radio. The junior medium of television would develop to rival radio later in the decade.

Radio reached into every home in the land, and simultaneously united the nation, an important factor during the Second World War. Broadcasting in Britain had begun formally in 1922 with the establishment of the British Broadcasting Company (BBC: it became the

Corporation in 1927), and until just before the outbreak of war was under the stern and authoritarian control of its first director-general, the Calvinistic Lord Reith whose fierce moral ethos lingered long after his departure. Reith abhorred American-style radio with its situation comedies and shows built around comic personalities, and the pre-war BBC was generally serious, sober and respectably middle-class. Even Reith was unable to hold back the tide forever, and in 1938 *Band Waggon*, a show modelled on American lines with Arthur Askey and Richard Murdoch in situation comedy sketches supported by Jack Hylton and his Band, took to the air and was an immediate, sensational success. In the following year *It's That Man Again*, which starred the Liverpool comedian Tommy Handley and an assortment of characters, was another milestone in the comic liberation of the British airwaves. Shortly after the launch of *ITMA* the Second World War started. For the benefit of the troops, transcribed shows from the United States were broadcast regularly for the first time by the BBC, and home audiences listened to Bob Hope, Jack Benny, and others, comparing them with the home-grown *ITMA*, and its rival *Hi Gang!* which featured the slick skills of three expatriate Americans, Bebe Daniels, Ben Lyon and Vic Oliver.

The war was to alter perceptions of radio comedy, and in the immediate period following it several shows started up that had derived from wartime entertainment, such as *Much-Binding-in-the-Marsh* with Richard Murdoch and Kenneth Horne, which sprang from the Royal Air Force component of *Merrygoround*, a weekly show featuring one of the three services each week.

A new generation of star performers emerged, many of whom had served in the forces. Charlie Chester, Eric Barker, Peter Sellers, Tony Hancock, Harry Secombe, Jon Pertwee, Spike

LEFT Televising the Cambridge Footlights 1962 show, *Double Take*, directed by Trevor Nunn. Miriam Margoyles is centre stage, Graham Chapman fourth from right

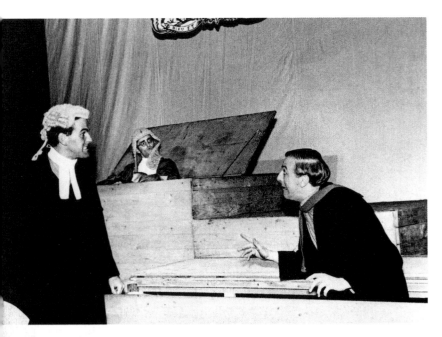

ABOVE **'Judge Not'** sketch: *Cambridge Circus* 1963, John Cleese, David Hatch and Graham Chapman

Milligan, Michael Bentine, Jimmy Edwards, Arthur Haynes and Max Bygraves were among those who made their mark in post-war radio. It is difficult to appreciate the impact of radio comedy on the British consciousness at that time. In 1949 Tommy Handley died suddenly, after ten consecutive seasons of *ITMA*. The scale of national mourning was only surpassed by the demise of the monarch, George VI, three years later.

Television, which had been introduced as the world's first high-definition service by the BBC in 1936, had been suspended throughout the war and did not return to the air until 1946, with transmissions limited to a thirty-mile radius of London and a handful of viewers who could afford the cost of receivers, then the equivalent of more than two months' national average wage. Towards the end of the decade a second transmitter was opened up in the Midlands, followed by another in the North, but the costs and limited programming restricted its appeal. The spectacle of the coronation of Elizabeth II in 1953 boosted the number of viewers, but the transformation into a popular medium was not to happen until the BBC's monopoly was broken in 1955, with the introduction of Independent Television (ITV). Throughout the 1950s radio still remained the dominant source of broadcast comedy, listened to avidly by schoolchildren of the period, including this writer and the future Pythons.

Two radio comedy shows in particular exercised a profound influence. The first was *Take It From Here*, scripted by Frank Muir and Denis Norden, which had moved into the Thursday evening time-slot occupied for so many years by *ITMA*. Its stars were the two Australians, Dick Bentley and Joy Nichols, with Jimmy Edwards, who at Cambridge had been a member of the Footlights revue club and had served in the RAF's Bomber Command, winning the DFC. If the hallmark of *Take It From Here* was its polished professionalism, *The Goon Show* by contrast represented dedicated anarchy. It had begun modestly as *Crazy People* in 1951, uniting the talents of Peter Sellers, who had made his name as an impressionist with Ted Ray on *Ray's a Laugh*, Harry Secombe who had followed Tony Hancock and Max Bygraves on *Educating Archie* as tutors to a ventriloquist's doll manipulated by Peter Brough (earlier in America Edgar Bergen had shown that ventriloquism could still work on radio) and two other comedians making a radio breakthrough, Michael Bentine and Spike Milligan. *The Goon Show* was manic and surreal, its virtue was its unpredictability, with each week an absurder plot trumping that

from the week before. It held a particular appeal for the young, and even the young heir to the throne, Prince Charles, was ensnared in its thrall.

At the beginning of the fifties there was still a respect for royalty and a deference to authority. The bulwarks of the British establishment – Parliament, the civil service, the judiciary, the church, the armed services, the public schools, the ancient universities of Oxford and Cambridge – occupied an unchallenged position. A Tory government replaced Clement Attlee's post-war Labour administration in 1951 and the political climate began to change. Rationing ceased in 1954, ITV began broadcasting in 1955. Materialism replaced austerity. The political cataclysm that began the shift in attitudes towards authority occurred in 1956 with Suez and the ill-considered British intervention, a debacle that even polarized the cabinet.

Cambridge was in the vanguard of change. A new breed of undergraduates held ambitions for careers in the arts and media, rather than the law and the civil service, and set about attaining their goals. Peter Hall and Trevor Nunn laid the foundation of their future pre-eminence in the small theatre belonging to the Amateur Dramatic Club on whose stage Bamber Gascoigne mounted his oddly titled revue *Share My Lettuce*, which transferred to a long West End run with Maggie Smith and Kenneth Williams while the author was still a

BELOW **Cambridge Footlights 1964: Eric Idle is in lower right foreground**

Magdalene undergraduate. Michael Frayn in his first term won a large prize in a copywriting competition held by the *Observer*, the first time his gift for comic writing was recognized with cash. In that same year the Footlights revue *Out of the Blue* had transferred to the Phoenix in the West End, and Fleet Street devoted many column inches to a twenty-year-old medical student whose wild appearance and manic movements were unsuitably compared with Danny Kaye's. It was the first time that the public became aware of the future Dr Jonathan Miller.

The Footlights are a Cambridge institution that has no exact Oxford equivalent. Founded in 1883, the club originally staged parochial musical comedies. Informal concerts known as 'smokers' were presented to all-male audiences within college walls. In this century, with punctuations for two world wars, the tradition has become established that during the university's post-

RIGHT *Cambridge Circus* on Broadway: Jonathan Lynn, Bill Oddie, David Hatch, foreground, John Cleese, Tim Brooke-Taylor, Graham Chapman

14

exam euphoria, the period known as May Week (which is actually a fortnight in June) the Footlights stage a show, usually in revue format. The female roles used to be taken by young males in drag, wearing rouge and mascara, and among the undergraduates drawn to the club between the wars were such future fashion luminaries as Norman Hartnell, Victor Stiebel and Cecil Beaton. In 1932 a precedent was set by allowing women to take part, gruffly abandoned in the following year when the show was called pointedly, *No More Women*. It would remain so until the 1957 revue *Zounds* by Michael Frayn, and from 1959 the barriers were lowered.

Several future stars appeared in the pre-war Footlights; among them Jack Hulbert, followed by his younger brother, Claude, Richard Murdoch and Jimmy Edwards. After the fifties it seemed that the main attraction the club offered was its direct route into show business, with for example, Hugh Laurie, Stephen Fry, Emma Thompson, Tony Slattery and Sandy Toksvig all contributing to the 1981 show, *The Cellar Tapes*. The 1959 show, *The Last Laugh*, directed by John Bird, was the first to take a sharply polemical post-Suez line, and was a precursor of the so-called satire movement, another invention of Fleet Street, which would spawn *Beyond the Fringe*, *That Was the Week That Was* compered by the ex-Footlight David Frost on BBC television, the Establishment nightclub in the West End and the satirical fortnightly journal, *Private Eye*. In *The Last Laugh* was Peter Cook, an Oxbridge humorist much influenced by the Goons, who had perfected a deadpan dull voice in his characterization of the raincoated nutter E L Wisty, apparently able to pontificate on any given topic *ad nauseam*. Cook could also effortlessly parody the dialogue of Harold Pinter – then the most vogueish playwright – and was invited by Michael Codron, the entrepreneur who had staged Gascoigne's *Share My Lettuce* in the West End, to write items for his revue *Pieces of Eight*, alongside the same Pinter. It was a success and was followed by a sequel, but Cook's irreverence had actually helped to kill off intimate revue, until then a popular mainstay of the West End theatre, with three or four usually running at any given time.

Edinburgh has long provided an accommodating platform for the university wits. During the period of the Festival the number of subsidiary, unofficial 'fringe' attractions running concurrently with main events can number into the hundreds. In 1960 a revue was

RIGHT **Graham
Chapman and David
Hatch in** *Cambridge
Circus,* **1963**

staged as part of the main programme at the suggestion of a recent Oxonian, John Bassett, who had become assistant to Robert Ponsonby, the Festival administrator. The cast consisted of two Oxford men, the owl-like Alan Bennett who had spent his National Service learning Russian and writing funny sketches with a fellow conscript, Michael Frayn, and Dudley Moore, a diminutive organ scholar at Magdalen who could play cool piano jazz and be fast with repartee. Balancing them were two others from Cambridge, Peter Cook, the reigning star of the Footlights, and Jonathan Miller, who had gone down four years earlier but whose lifelong alternation between medicine and the stage had already suggested serious schizoid tendencies. The title, *Beyond the Fringe* – which then had an apt meaning – has long since become as arcane as *A Clockwork Orange* but the show, plainly staged without scenery and few props became a watershed in British comedy, mixing considerable doses of political satire, with Peter Cook delivering a memorable impersonation of the prime minister, Harold Macmillan lecturing the nation on how to behave during a nuclear attack. *Beyond the Fringe* set out to demythologize the Establishment viewpoint, and British war films and even Shakespeare came in for lampooning. The show satisfied both critics and audiences, and was transferred to the West End for a long run at the Fortune Theatre, where the prime minister made a point of seeing himself caricatured, and bore it with customary good humour. The quartet of young men suddenly found themselves famous and in 1962 re-staged it on Broadway where its Britishness in a town accustomed to the very different humorous approach of Mike Nichols and Elaine May, Bob Newhart and Shelley Berman still drew acclamation. *Beyond the Fringe* was the Broadway show that had to be seen.

Its acceptance was pivotal in shaping the careers of the funny-men who followed. Cook started the Establishment nightclub in Soho, having taken the idea from the satirical cabarets he had visited in Germany during the year between leaving school and going to Cambridge, intending it to be a place where the literati could meet, eat and savour biting entertainment. It attracted considerable attention when the persecuted American comedian Lenny Bruce appeared, together with a large contingent of members of Scotland Yard's Special Branch. The Establishment's heyday was brief. After two years financial control passed to other hands and it

ended up as a tacky drinking club. Cook had more success with the periodical *Private Eye*, which persists to this day. He was the majority shareholder of the satirical fortnightly which was launched by Richard Ingrams who had been at Oxford, Christopher Booker who had been at Cambridge, and William Rushton.

Booker and Rushton were also contributors to *That Was the Week That Was*, the irreverent BBC satire show which in 1962 was unlike anything previously seen on television, a Brechtian-revue format show with little scenery and cameras and technicians frequently in shot, which interspersed sketches and comedy numbers with fierce and deadly serious attacks on living people. It was regarded with discomfort in the upper echelons of the BBC and enjoyed a brief, short life, coming off the air for ever in good time for the 1964 general election.

LEFT **David Frost with** ***Frost Over England*** **cast, 1967: Julie Felix, Sheila Steafel, Ronnie Barker, John Cleese, Ronnie Corbett**

TW3 was very much a writers' show, and a name that occasionally appeared in the end credits was that of John Cleese, a towering (6'4") presence in the 1963 Footlights revue, *A Clump of Plinths*, directed by Humphrey Barclay, who would become a prime force in television comedy production. The show was imported into the West End by Michael White as *Cambridge Circus*, and among the other performers were Bill Oddie, Tim Brooke-Taylor, David Hatch, Jo Kendall and Graham Chapman, a former Cambridge medical student furthering his studies at St Bartholomew's Hospital. Barclay gained a job at the BBC and gathered the cast for three radio programmes featuring a mixture of old and new material, called *I'm Sorry, I'll Read That Again*. In the following year, 1964, Michael White took *Cambridge Circus* on a tour of New Zealand, Chapman delaying his qualification as a doctor in order to go. He claimed that the Queen Mother on a visit to Bart's had persuaded him: 'It's a beautiful place – you must go.' It was a gruelling tour, requiring hard work to persuade audiences to laugh. While they were there an offer came from the veteran producer Sol Hurok to stage the show on Broadway.

BELOW *Do Not Adjust Your Set*, with Terry Jones, Michael Palin, David Jason and Eric Idle

Oxford, without the Footlights, nevertheless had its theatrical strengths. The Experimental Theatre Club sent revues to Edinburgh, and among the talents sharpened in the early sixties were Michael York, Miles Kington, Diana Quick, Braham Murray and Clare Francis, but notably Michael Palin and Terry Jones. Both of them appeared in the ETC's sub-Brechtian diatribe against capital punishment called *Hang Down Your Head and Die* in which clowns and girls in fishnet tights mimed grisly re-enactments of executions, and it played in the West End.

Palin and Jones continued their collaboration in *The Oxford Revue* at Edinburgh in 1964. After they had gone down – Jones in 1964, Palin in 1965 – they found themselves writing scripts for *The Frost Report* alongside John Cleese, Graham

Chapman and a later Cambridge Footlight, Eric Idle. Five of the six future Pythons were now within the same frame, at the instigation of David Frost, and were invited by him to write the 'Continuous Developing Monologue' with which he fronted the show. Frost then produced a series called *At Last the 1948 Show* for ITV with Cleese, Chapman, Tim Brooke-Taylor and the pop-eyed writer-comedian Marty Feldman writing and performing. Idle, Palin and Jones then worked on a show, *Do Not Adjust Your Set*, for Humphrey Barclay who had become a producer at Rediffusion, then the weekday London ITV contractor. Cleese and Chapman wrote the first programme in a series based on Richard Gordon's *Doctor in the House* and Jones and Palin *The Complete and Utter History of Britain*, a spoof historical series which went largely unnoticed.

Barry Took, who with Feldman had written scripts for the brilliant radio show *Round the Horne*, was now a comedy producer and advisor at the BBC, and had the idea of uniting Cleese, Chapman, Palin, Jones and Idle. He also remembered a young American who had demonstrated an extraordinary talent as a lighting artist in front of the camera on a Humphrey Barclay programme, *We Have Ways of Making You Laugh*, and who could construct simple but effective animations as well. He was Terry Gilliam, destined to become the sixth Python. Said Took: 'I had admired Cleese and Chapman, and Palin and Jones. What I had in mind was that Michael Palin and John Cleese should work together – that I thought would be a magic combination. But it was really "love me, love my dog". They said they would like the others and Eric Idle. So that was duly arranged. But the BBC was terribly worried about these people. When I met them, and saw how they interplayed – the irritation, the refusal to give an inch, the fact that some came from Oxford and some from Cambridge – I saw that it was absolutely right and to the point.'

It was the spark that set the Pythons alight. Cleese remembers that it was he and Chapman who approached the BBC with an idea after *Do Not Adjust Your Set* with Jones and Palin, and that they were referred on to Barry Took. He feels therefore, that the inspiration came as much from the future Pythons themselves as it did from Took. Whichever way it happened, it has to be regarded as a divine moment in the history of British comedy.

REDIFFUSION LONDON invites you to meet DENISE COFFEY · ERIC IDLE · DAVID JASON · TERRY JONES · MIKE PALIN and the BONZO DOG DOO-DAH BAND

AUDIENCE

Monday 6 November

DO NOT ADJUST YOUR SET

The Fairly Pointless Show

ADMIT ONE

DO NOT ADJUST YOUR SET

INSTRUCTIONS FOR AUDIENCE

1. Do not adjust your parents.
2. Place them tidily in front of the Television Set.
3. Do not play with them.
4. Give them a bone to chew and come to Rediffusion Television Studios, Wembley on Monday, November 6th, 1967 (8.30 - 9.15 p.m. Doors open 8.00 - 8.15 p.m.)
5. Laugh.

This ticket admits ONE PERSON (provided he or she is 10 or over)

LEFT *Admission ticket for a recording of* Do Not Adjust Your Set, 1967

19

MICHAEL PALIN

BORN 5TH MAY 1943
SHEFFIELD
YORKSHIRE

Given a tendency to attach labels to each member of a group, the one usually applied to Michael Palin as a Python is that he is 'the nice one.' With remarkable patience and not a little frustration he has done his best to dispel it, even by taking the path to almost inevitable public opprobrium by becoming a television superstar. Yet that route would seem to have failed. In spite of his circumnavigation of the world attended by a film crew, his journey from one polar region to the other and his sojourn in the Isle of Wight, he remains as nice as ever.

He is the youngest Python, but only by a few weeks. He was born in Sheffield on 5 May 1943, a mere five weeks after Eric Idle. A Yorkshireman by birth and upbringing, he has absorbed certain traditional northern prejudices such as that people should not live in Surrey. His father was an engineer, spending almost his entire working life with Edgar Allen and Company, one of the several steel manufacturers that gave Sheffield its place in the world. Michael followed his sister Angela into the world by a gap of nine years, and spent his childhood in a large Victorian house, solidly built in the local stone, at Ranmoor on the Pennines side of the city.

It was a happy childhood. 'My father was quite strict. He was insistent on things like mealtimes – lunch had to be exactly at ten-past-one, supper at exactly twenty-past-seven. He didn't like me bringing friends home in the evening, which was quite hard because I was fairly gregarious. I used to spend a great deal of time next door with a chap called Graham Stewart-Harris, who still lives in Sheffield – his father was a doctor, and they had a far more easy-going regime in their house. We had a very regular existence. Two weeks holiday in the summer where we went to one or two places, either Sheringham in Norfolk or Southwold in Suffolk.

*Palin in **Ripping Yarns***

ABOVE Birkdale Preparatory School 1956
cricket XI. Michael Palin (scorer) is back
row, right

Creature of habit, my father was. The house was in the better part of Sheffield, but it was rented, it wasn't owned. My father didn't really earn a great deal of money. I was surprised after he died and I found out how much he had been earning when he sent me away to public school. It must have cost about a third of his income. What I saw as parsimony was really the result of necessity – we couldn't afford exotic holidays. I remember we got our television eight or nine years after the Stewart-Harrisses, for instance.'

The expensive establishment was Shrewsbury, his father's old school. Shrewsbury has a

ABOVE **Michael Palin as the cooper's apprentice in Terry Gilliam's Jabberwocky**

special place in the evolution of British humour in the latter half of the twentieth century, being the nursery for Peter Cook, Christopher Booker, Richard Ingrams and William Rushton, the founding fathers of *Private Eye*, the satirical fortnightly magazine. They were a few years ahead of Michael, who never got beyond submitting an occasional match report to *The Salopian*, the traditional school magazine. 'There was a lot of sport at school. I remember being permanently cold and short of breath, and carrying vast amounts of books from our house to the main school buildings, taking care not to walk over certain parts of the grounds that you couldn't step on until you had been there for four years. Shrewsbury was a great home for elaborate practical jokes. Even the masters would play them on one another. Our house was a very happy one, largely due to a wonderful housemaster who kept us full of laughter, and enabled us to cope with the awful food and waking up in winter with six inches of snow on our beds.'

He did not go on to Clare, his father's college at Cambridge, but instead went to Oxford. 'I wasn't scholarship material but the school thought that I should have a go, since it would help me get a place. I went up for the Magdalen and Worcester exams, and they gave me some of the most embarrassing moments of my life. I wanted to read English, and I had mugged up on Graham Greene, still one of my favourite authors. They asked what authors I had read, and when I said Greene, they said no, no, authors on the syllabus. It was then that I realized English at Oxford stopped in 1900. So I tried to get out of it by saying I liked poetry. They asked me, whose poetry? You know how it is when you are on the run – your mind seizes up. I

FROGS KEEP MOIST

LEFT **Denholm Elliott and Michael Palin in** *Across the Andes by Frog* **from the Ripping Yarns series, 1977**

23

couldn't think of anyone. After a long pause I said "Wordsworth." The man must have scented blood because he said "Name six of his poems." After another forty seconds I said "Michael", then eventually I muttered "Daffodils". Well, that was Worcester. And then for the Magdalen exam I can remember getting a general paper which had a quote on it, "A house is a machine for living in – Le Corbusier. Discuss." And I can remember starting "Of course this was all right when Le Corbusier lived in the sixteenth century, but now things are very different." In the end I got in to Brasenose, I'm not sure why. And I read History, which was safer.'

Having gained his place at Oxford, he left school with two terms to spare and filled in the time by working in the publicity department of his father's Sheffield firm. He had in his time at Shrewsbury begun to write humorous pieces, his housemaster encouraging the development of his talent, and now he started to insert funny articles in the works magazine. He also joined an amateur dramatic group, the Brightside and Carbrook Co-operative Society Players. 'We did heavy acting – a play called The *Woodcarver* about a realist carving of a statue of Christ for instance – and I remember doing a love scene on a couch with a lady who was seven months pregnant. My father didn't want me to be an actor, apart from very small parts in school plays. I think he thought it would interfere with my work. My sister joined a professional repertory company, and I know he would have preferred her to be a secretary. But he didn't mind me acting after I had left school because I had got my place at Oxford.

'Oxford was a revelation. There was so much freedom, so many things to do. I started off going in for sport, but then I realized how miserable it was, playing football in the cold, so after a few weeks I faded out. I made friends with Robert Hewison, who I suppose influenced me more than anyone else. He was a sort of urbane, smooth sophisticate from London and a bit of a joker, rather good at telling stories, and putting on funny voices, and I could see there was going to be trouble there, opposition. So if you can't beat 'em, join 'em. Robert and I became very good friends, and it was an opening for me into a quite different world. He was the driving force behind getting me to join OUDS and to start writing down the little comedy improvisations we used to do up in his room.'

They were both authorities on radio and television comedy and tried writing sketches for college revue groups, but they keenly felt the absence in Oxford of an organization to channel comedy writing in the way that the Footlights was able to at Cambridge. 'Robert was ambitious, and whereas

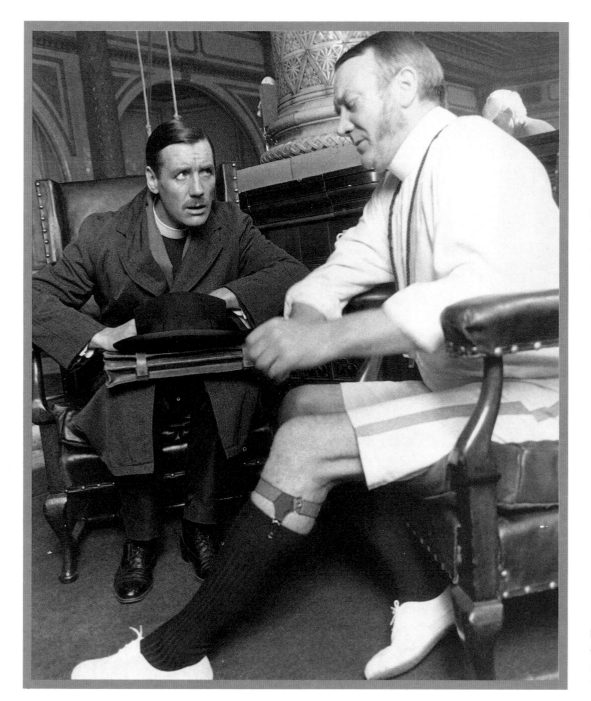

LEFT Michael Palin with Denholm Elliott as the bishop in *The Missionary*, 1982

FAR LEFT As Gordon Ottershaw in *Golden Gordon* from *Ripping Yarns*, 1979

25

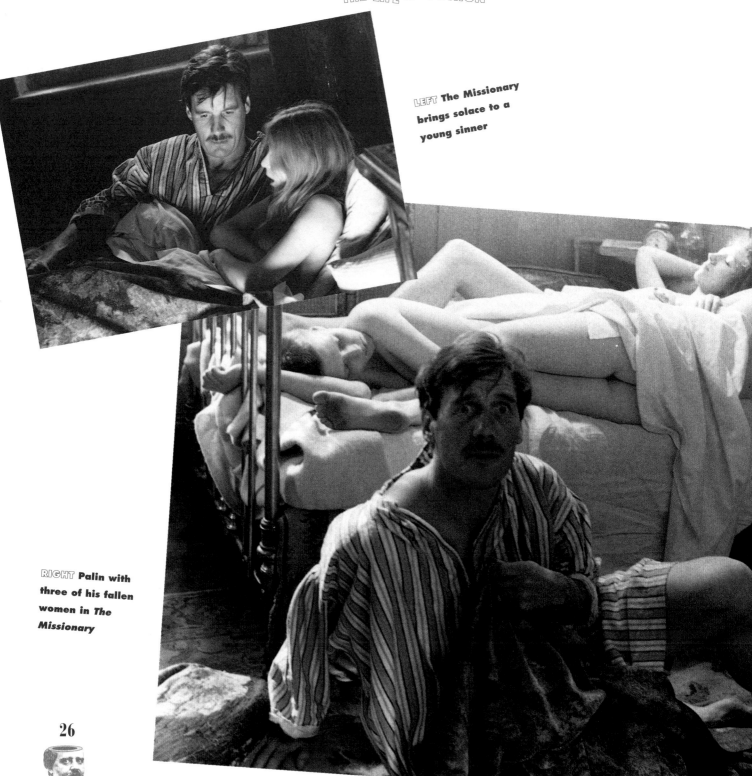

LEFT **The Missionary brings solace to a young sinner**

RIGHT **Palin with three of his fallen women in** *The Missionary*

26

my friends tended to be unfashionable, he used to get to know those who were successful. That's how I met Terry Jones, who was quite a well-known Oxford figure. He used to have an amazing dark-brown, hairy check coat, I remember, and he was tanned and dark, not pink-cheeked like I was. He had his own set-up at Teddy Hall, was much involved in the ETC plays that Michael Rudman did, and Brecht, the big thing then. Terry was definitely in the senior league. The first time we wrote together was for a show in a marquee called *Loitering Within Tent*.'

LEFT Michael Palin as The Missionary

Hewison was also responsible for the great romance in Michael Palin's life. 'I'd met Helen on holiday when I was quite young, about sixteen – it was a teenage holiday romance – and then I didn't see her for a long time. She lived in Cambridgeshire. She wrote me a note saying that she had heard that I had got into Oxford, and that they must have lowered their standards – something sarcastic like that – and that was all. Then Robert said that I must meet his girlfriend, called Piglet, who was in London at a teachers' training college, and it turned out to be the one at which Helen was also studying. So the girls came up to Oxford together. We were married in 1966, a year after I had left the university.'

In his second year there he had moved towards straight acting, appearing in an ETC production of Pinter's *The Birthday Party*. He also wrote some of the material and performed in the Brechtian revue attacking capital punishment, *Hang Down Your Head and Die* which transferred after Oxford to the Comedy Theatre in the West End for a six-week season. 'That was the first time that I felt that there was a chance that I could earn my living as an actor or a writer or both.'

During that summer of 1964, with Terry Jones, Nigel Pegram, Doug Fisher, and Annabel Leventon, he went to Edinburgh with *The Oxford Revue*. Terry Jones had by then gone down, but Michael Palin still had another year at Oxford, and finished his time off with *The Oxford Line*, a revue that moved even closer to surrealism, and managed to get a second in Modern History. Terry Jones, a year ahead in London, enlisted his help in writing an abortive musical on the theme of love for Willie Donaldson. Palin then landed a job at TWW, the Bristol-based ITV contractor which was soon to lose its franchise, as the anchorman on a teenage pop show called *Now*. The six-month stint furnished him with sufficient income to

27

dissuade him from taking up a regular job as an advertising copywriter, as well as providing the experience of facing a live studio camera.

He and Terry Jones were meanwhile performing cabaret in places like the Rehearsal Club, placing them in the line of vision of David Frost, who was on the hunt for writers for his new BBC series *The Frost Report*. Frost cemented his writing partnership with Terry Jones, which led to *A Series of Bird's* with John Bird and John Fortune and *Twice a Fortnight*, another Footlights-dominated show, with Bill Oddie, Jonathan Lynn and Graeme Garden, and Tony Palmer as producer. Terry Jones then ensured that Humphrey Barclay included Palin in *Do Not Adjust Your Set*, and they joined Eric Idle, David Jason and Denise Coffey. Barclay also produced Jones and Palin's spoof historical series *The Complete and Utter History of Britain* which they wrote in its entirety and performed in. There was also a television special in which Michael Palin appeared, called *How to Irritate People*, which was written by John Cleese and Graham Chapman.

Ultimately the call came from Barry Took to meet and arrange the comedy show that would become *Monty Python*. 'We all submerged our idiosyncrasies during the first series, and were rather polite to one another,' Palin recalls. Unlike the volatile Terry Jones, he is by nature equable and reflective and was able to evade clashes with the crushingly frank John Cleese. Jones and Palin, both influenced by Spike Milligan's *Q5* which had totally ignored the accepted conventions of television comedy, were able to impose the unstructured format on *Python* and found that Terry Gilliam was on their side. With gritted teeth the Cambridge men endured the dreadful locations, hideously itchy costumes and sundry other discomforts for the sake of the filmed inserts. Gilliam shared with Jones and Palin a fascination

for the distant past of Chaucer and King Arthur, and all its concomitant muckiness.

It was Michael's interest in the Arthurian legend that inspired the first true *Monty Python* film, *Monty Python and the Holy Grail.* An outline had been concocted in which the Grail was going to be found in Harrod's in a deliberate confusion of past and present, but after a number of screenplay sessions and discussions with all six Pythons, the modern intrusions, apart from verbal anachronisms were limited to the arrival of a police squad car and its occupants at the Scottish location near the end of the film, resulting in the arrests of some of the cast. Scotland turned out to be very rugged.

'There was a straight Oxford and Cambridge split. Oxford people can put up with far more discomfort. The Cambridge people cannot intellectually justify why they should be so uncomfortable when they could be just as funny in the studio. Terry and I always felt that we needed something extra, perhaps due to some deep-seated inadequacy in ourselves. That's always the way it was. I used sometimes to get cross privately that everyone wasn't pulling their weight with things like finishing off a recording session, or seeing how a bit of dubbing was coming along, things that didn't need everybody. The only two who could ever be contacted were Terry Jones and me because we were at home.

BELOW **Trevor Howard and Maggie Smith on a Scottish grouse moor with Michael Palin in** *The Missionary*

'But in a way it works out. It would be absolutely disastrous if we were all the same and did the same amount of work and never grumbled. It would have been awful. The centrifugal feeling that *Python* had was terribly important. It might have gone too far – everyone having gone off to areas of their own.'

Palin achieved considerable success outside the group, both by himself and in partnership with Terry Jones. They concocted a television comedy called *Tomkinson's Schooldays*, a parody of an Edwardian boarding-school story which led to a series being commissioned by Terry

Hughes, called *Ripping Yarns*. It was filmed rather than taped, and the subject matter of each tale varied. The titles, *The Testing of Eric Olthwaite*, *Escape from Stalag Luft 112B*, *Murder at Moorstones Manor*, *Across the Andes by Frog*, *The Curse of the Claw*, and in the second series, *Golden Gordon*, *Whinfrey's Last Case* and *Roger of the Raj*, convey the affectionate tone in which various sub-divisions of old-fashioned juvenile literature were treated.

He also played the Candide-like hero of Terry Gilliam's film *Jabberwocky*, as the cooper's apprentice who is mistaken for a prince and is obliged to rid the kingdom of the dreadful dragon that has been menacing it. Later he co-wrote and appeared in Gilliam's next film, *Time Bandits*, in a minor role with Shelley Duvall, both playing a pair of lovers whose affair seems to continue through several historical eras.

The next film he wrote was *The Missionary*, which he also co-produced and starred in, as a churchman returning to Edwardian England after many years in the African bush preaching the gospel. At his bishop's insistence he establishes a refuge for fallen women in the East End, and is then seduced by the wife of a bloodthirsty senile peer and she bankrolls his endeavours. Directed by Richard Loncraine, with a brilliant cast that included Maggie Smith, Denholm Elliott, Trevor Howard, David Suchet and, as an extraordinarily decrepit absent-minded butler, Michael Hordern, the film suffered in some respects from a super-abundance of ideas that muddled its flow.

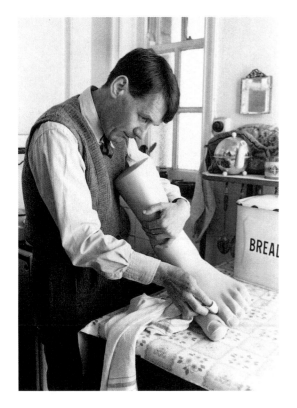

BELOW **Palin in
A Private Function,
1984**

Palin next appeared as the lead in *A Private Function*, directed by Malcolm Mowbray and written by Alan Bennett, a comedy set in early postwar Yorkshire during the period of intense food rationing. It enabled him to extend his acting range. 'He is the only actor among us,' said Terry Gilliam, 'the rest of us are just caricaturists,' and to prove his point he put him in a downbeat role as a sinister interrogator in his black comedy of a bleak future, *Brazil*, for once a nasty character. In the most successful post-Python film, *A Fish Called Wanda*, he played Ken Pile, a small-time crook and animal-loving member of Kevin Kline and Jamie Lee Curtis's gang. John Cleese asked him to play the part with a stammer, inadvertently causing protests from organizations protecting the interests of sufferers, but Palin worked hard to make it clear that there was no malicious mockery involved, and eventually they were mollified.

His most personal work in the cinema was the writing of and performing in a film called *American Friends*, which was directed by Tristram Powell and co-starred Trini Alvarado and Connie Booth. The story was based on a Palin family memoir which he had discovered, the diary of a Victorian ancestor who had been an Oxford don in mid-Victorian times and had fallen in love with a young American

girl while on a walking holiday in the Alps. At that time Oxford colleges were still run like religious houses and dons were not allowed to marry. Palin's great-grandfather threw up his chance of becoming the head of his college, married the girl and spent the rest of his life in happiness as a country vicar. The film was a love story, a romance against the odds, and a triumph over narrow bigotry. Sensitively acted and shot in appropriate locations, it deserved a wider release, and unseen was in America in spite of the obvious connection.

Palin's television work has included a couple of teleplays that also sprang from his past. The Screen Two production of *East of Ipswich*, broadcast early in 1987, was based on a family holiday in Suffolk in the 1950s, the one in which he had met his future wife. Originally it had been intended for the David Puttnam First Love series on Channel 4 but that series came to an end before it was ready, so it passed to the BBC. *East of Ipswich* was followed by *Number 27*, which attacked the prevailing Yuppie mentality of buying up properties as a means of boosting assets without accepting the responsibility of making them habitable. It went out on BBC1 in October 1988.

In 1991 he played a leading role in a seven-part Channel 4 serial by Alan Bleasdale, called *GBH*. He played the head of a school for physically disadvantaged children who is targeted by the militant thugs surrounding an ambitious, megalomaniacal local politician, played by Robert Lindsay. The

RIGHT **Rest break for the cast in *A Private Function***

conflict arises from the teacher's decision to stay at his post on a day in which all council employees have been called out on strike. A tough, realistic drama, based on militancy in Liverpool local government in the 1980s, it excited a great deal of public attention and critical praise. Originally Palin had been offered the Lindsay part, but was perfectly content when the roles were switched.

Alas, not everything he has done has been an unalloyed success. He and Terry Jones wrote a play called *Secrets* for the BBC, which was aired in 1973. There was some interest in turning it into a film, and even attempts by other writers to produce a script based on it. In 1985 Jones and Palin were asked by Samuel Goldwyn Jr to write a film script. It eventually became *Consuming Passions*, directed by Giles Foster, with the writing credits going to Paul D Zimmerman and Andrew Davies. Critics hated it, and the public stayed away. Palin and Jones could at least comfort themselves that the screenplay was no longer recognizably theirs.

No such excuses were available in 1994 when Palin's first stage play, *The Weekend*, opened in the West End, with Richard Wilson and Angela Thorne in the leads. The reviews were

32

LEFT Michael Palin with Trini Alvarado and Connie Booth in *American Friends*, 1991

A tale of murder, greed, lust, revenge and seafood.

JOHN CLEESE

JAMIE LEE CURTIS

KEVIN KLINE

MICHAEL PALIN

METRO-GOLDWYN-MAYER Presents
A MICHAEL SHAMBERG/PROMINENT FEATURES Production "A FISH CALLED WANDA"
Starring JOHN CLEESE · JAMIE LEE CURTIS · KEVIN KLINE · MICHAEL PALIN Story by JOHN CLEESE & CHARLES CRICHTON
Executive Producer STEVE ABBOTT & JOHN CLEESE Produced by MICHAEL SHAMBERG Directed by CHARLES CRICHTON
Screenplay by JOHN CLEESE © 1988 METRO-GOLDWYN-MAYER PICTURES, INC. IN ASSOCIATION WITH STAR PARTNERS LIMITED

A FISH CALLED WANDA

discouraging, noting that the quarrelsome, complaining character played by Wilson bore some kinship with his Victor Meldrew characterization in the sitcom *One Foot in the Grave*, and that the plotting was like Alan Ayckbourn at half-tempo. John Peter, the distinguished critic of *The Sunday Times* said: 'I admire Palin's work as much as the next man, but I bet you anything, if this play had been written by you or me, it would never have got within shouting distance of a regional rep, let alone the West End. It's as if television success entitled you to any other kind of success.' Palin promised to try harder next time.

One of his enthusiasms is travel, particularly by train, and in 1980 he leapt at an opportunity offered by the BBC to participate in its documentary series *Great Railway Journeys of the World*. Most of the other travellers who were taking part, such as Michael Frayn and Ludovic Kennedy, opted for the exotic or vast distances, across Australia, the United States and China. Palin preferred something nearer home and journeyed from Euston to the Kyle of Lochalsh on the West Coast of Scotland, even encountering some steam, with the preserved *Flying Scotsman* locomotive pulling his train. Palin's pleasant manner and almost Betjemanesque relish for the sights encountered resulted in one of the most popular programmes in the series. He was remembered later when the BBC had the idea to retrace Phileas Fogg's circumnavigation, *Around the World in 80 Days*. The proviso was that only methods of transportation available in Jules Verne's day would be permitted – trains, boats and horse-drawn vehicles – although strikes and other unforeseen problems required him to board the occasional bus. It was a hugely popular series, and in spite of the artificiality of travelling around attended by a film crew Palin made every stage of it look spontaneous. In fact, the pre-planning often collapsed when connections were cancelled, and there was cliff-hanging suspense to the very end when Palin finally made it back to the Reform Club at the last moment. A bestselling book recounting his adventures quickly followed.

The idea was so successful that an ingenious sequel was proposed on the basis of 'We've done across, now let's go down'. The result was *Pole to Pole*, actually a far more arduous journey – Palin cracked a rib on the Zambezi rapids – which extended over five months, some of them spent in hideous climactic conditions. The journey began at the northernmost point of Norway and continued through to the South Pole. The North Pole was reached later during the short window of the year in which it is safe to go there. But another successful television series resulted as well as a bestseller based on his diary of the trip. He has an almost obsessive need to keep his life in order, and writing a daily journal is one of the ways in which he fulfils it. When he feels the time is ripe for his autobiography he will not be short of original material, but there will be a colossal problem when it comes to boiling it down.

The Palins live in Oak Village, a pretty Victorian enclave near Gospel Oak station, south of Hampstead Heath. Originally their home was tiny, but the house has been enlarged by first the acquisition of another which backed on to the same internal courtyard, and then the house adjoining. It was thus possible to make reasonable space available for their three children, sons Thomas and William and daughter Rachel, plus the two cats, Betty and Albert. Palin's study is located in a converted loft, a bright studio room with a terrace, and he enjoys working in it, particularly the planning of his journeys. 'I like to organize projects where I can go to all the places I dreamed about when I was a child.'

Appropriately, in 1986 he was made chairman of Transport 2000, a pressure group responsible for lobbying for better public transportation and an abandonment of unnecessary road schemes. He was a 'green' long before a political party appropriated the name, and is as concerned for his local environment as Terry Jones, at the opposite point of the London compass in Grove Park, is devoted to his. They have much more in common than the other Pythons, not just their Oxford backgrounds, but that they are both concerned ecologists who involve themselves in practical causes. They are also both authors of children's books, and they dabble from time to time in journalism. Lacking the abrasive and pragmatic characteristics of the hard-headed Cambridge men, they are much more likely to win points for their astonishing niceness.

BELOW As headteacher of a special school in Alan Bleasdale's Channel 4 drama series, *GBH*

35

TERRY JONES

All the Pythons have an eclectic range of talents; Terry Jones in particular is hard to compartmentalize. His range of enthusiasms is breathtaking. Speak to him on fossil fuels, or Rupert Bear, or mercenaries in the Middle Ages or modern China and in a moment you will find yourself hopelessly out of your depth, floored by his knowledge. Not that he is a show-off. His is a good-natured enthusiasm which he tries to communicate to others. Some of the other Pythons see themselves as tired old cynics in comparison, and have even resented his unflagging loyalty to the preservation of the group as a continuing unit. He is of Python's Oxford contingent, one of John Cleese's woolly romantics. He is warm and funny, with a sharp appreciation for the ridiculous, but he is not a cynic. His energies are directed at making sense of daily existence.

'It's the Welsh blood, you see,' he says, 'we're all so terribly enthusiastic. In a Welsh accent, if you make a suggestion you get excited at the end of a sentence, but if you make a suggestion in a Surrey accent you go down at the end of the sentence, and it comes out hard, as though you are laying down the law. I realized some years ago that people sometimes find me hard to take – even my wife has said I can be very dominating.' The contrast in the geography could well be that of Neil Kinnock and John Major, the contenders in the 1992 general election, which resulted in the latter's victory. Politically Terry Jones was on the side of the former and the sense of Welsh kinship was strong. Yet in spite of that there's a fundamental inconsistency in his background.

Terry Jones was born in Colwyn Bay, a pleasant resort on the North Wales coast, on 1 February 1942. His father was a native of the area, but his mother came from Bolton in the industrial heartland of Lancashire. 'My father always wanted to be a carpenter but he was a bank clerk all his life, one of the great wastes – it was regarded as a good

BORN 1ST FEBRUARY 1942
COLWYN BAY
NORTH WALES

RIGHT **Echoing his schooldays in *The Meaning of Life***

36

The Guildford Royal Grammar School 1st XV,
1960, Terry Jones holding the ball

steady job during the depression. When he eventually retired he became a changed man and started living for the first time.' His father's only break from Barclay's Bank occurred during the Second World War when he served in the Royal Air Force and went to India. After the war the family – which included Nigel, Terry's older brother by two years – moved to Claygate in Surrey.

'It scarred me for life, and I spent fifteen years going around saying I was Welsh, hating this place we had moved to in commuter Surrey, away from Colwyn Bay with its beach and Fairy Glen and Iris Park. We lived in a little semi-detached house, and as I was five I went to the local Church of England primary school. From about the age of six I was going to be a poet – my first poem was called "Prairie Fires" if I remember right. I never read anything then. I went on to the Royal Grammar School at Guildford.'

RIGHT **Gladys (Graham Chapman) and George (Terry Jones) watch a documentary on molluscs**

His enthusiasm at the RGS earned him the captaincy of the rugby 1st XV and he was also a prominent member of the school Corps. He believes he was something of a goody-goody, 'Any work I was given I automatically did. I suppose I was a bit of a swot, although I didn't mean to be.' He was, to his chagrin, unable to perform. 'The headmaster felt that actors were by definition homosexuals and communists. I can remember him giving us a lecture on homosexuality in which he said the sure sign of one was green suede shoes. I have never worn them since.'

In the breaks while doing his homework he listened to radio comedy and *The Goon Show* proved to have a profound influence on his outlook. As a child he could even remember

38

listening to *ITMA*. 'I was also keen on *Up the Pole* with Jimmy Jewel and Ben Warris, and *Much-Binding-in-the-Marsh* with Richard Murdoch and Kenneth Horne. I've always been a sparse reader, though. I used to go to the movies. I remember seeing Danny Kaye pulling faces and deciding that I could do that, and I wanted to be a film star. That is, apart from a short period, after which I thought I would like to be a classical composer – for about three days. I didn't watch television very much but I remember greatly enjoying Michael Bentine's *It's a Square World* because he was using the medium to produce visual humour. But I suppose it was Jacques Tati who really got me going on that.'

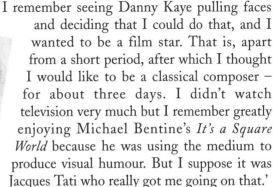

He found that not only did he dislike mathematics but suffered from a general allergy towards the sciences. English was the subject at which he excelled. Even so, he nearly destroyed his A-level chances by misreading the examination instructions, and completing four essays on Shakespeare when only two were required for marking, which left him no time to deal with the rest of the paper. He spent a third year in the sixth form, failing to be accepted by a number of universities – Exeter, Bristol, London, Manchester. He went to Cambridge to be interviewed by Gonville and Caius College, was described as a mixture of simplicity and sophistication, and invited to take their entrance examination. He also underwent the exam for St Edmund Hall, Oxford. 'I didn't really want to go to Teddy Hall. I didn't want to do Latin and Anglo-Saxon. Caius would have been very exciting, where my tutor would have been Donald Davie who contributed poetry to the *New Statesman*. But I was offered a place at Teddy Hall. Then a week after I had accepted I was offered one at Caius. The school put pressure on me not to change. So I went to Oxford.'

The chronology of the receipt of the two letters was the fortuitous accident that determined the constitution of *Monty Python*. Had Terry Jones gone to Cambridge he is absolutely sure he would never have had the nerve to go near the Footlights, which seemed to him extremely well organized.

He went up to Oxford in 1961. 'I was very impressed by the corduroy suits, a sign of rebellion in those days. I was very intimidated by the place in my first year, and it took me three years to find out that it wasn't quite as impressive as I thought it was going to be.' The deciphering of *Beowulf* aside, he found reading English very satisfying and was particularly interested in Middle English. 'Even at school I'd had quite a strong pull towards Chaucer – I felt that he was a good guy, and my admiration for him has been growing ever since.

'I got into the theatre scene via the college show, really. Even at school we had done a little, such as end of term revues – I remember getting all the prefects to do a chicken chorus. But at Teddy Hall there was a sudden intake of Thespians. We had Michael Rudman that year reading English and he quickly took over the college drama society. I was in his first production. I then found myself doing little funny roles. In my second year I did a review. Ian Davidson, Doug Fisher and Robin Grove-White had done one the year before with Paul McDowell and were going up to Edinburgh with it, but Paul suddenly had a hit song, *You're Driving Me Crazy* which he recorded with the Temperance Seven, and it was taking up all of his time so I was asked to go instead. It was pretty successful that year and came down to London first at the LAMDA theatre, then at the Phoenix. It was called ****[four asterisks]. When I went back for my third year I had a certain cachet because I had been on the West End stage, and suddenly everybody wanted me to be in their production. I eventually decided to do this thing with Braham Murray for the Experimental Theatre Club called *Hang Down Your Head and Die*, about capital punishment. We spent two terms preparing – it was going to be total theatre and everybody was going to write it. Michael Palin was in it as well. I had met him just a bit before. We were appalled at the final script that was produced – it was much too long and we were all panicking. I remember – the first time I wrote with Mike – he and Robert Hewison and I stayed up all one night and went through the show and organized it and went to Braham, but didn't meet with much approval at that stage. How it got on I don't know, but we did it.'

His time at Oxford was full. 'I worked on *Isis*, the undergraduate magazine, designing it, and I rather envied Cambridge's expertise in that area. I was laying out *Isis* in the morning, rehearsing some play in the afternoon and in the evenings I usually did a bit of reading. Typical Oxford days.'

Money, however, was a problem. His parents were unable to augment his meagre means-tested grant and during his vacations he

BELOW **Rather than hire women, the Pythons always tried to play the female roles themselves**

The lupins sketch from
Monty Python, with
Michael Palin

ABOVE Terry as the Naked Organist, a *Python* icon

had to work at a number of menial jobs including picking up household refuse for the Esher Urban District council. 'It was a wonderful atmosphere – there was a tremendous *esprit de corps* among the dustmen. You could tell what day of the week it was by what road you were in, and the time of day by where you were in that road. I came away with a new perception. I started looking at houses in a new way. Normally you look at the front door. But after two weeks of dustbins I was looking for the side door. The whole house was orientated around the dustbin.'

After *Hang Down Your Head and Die* he had only one term left to take his degree examinations, and then he went to Edinburgh to stage a revue with the Oxford Theatre Group which included Michael Palin, Doug Fisher, Nigel Pegram and Annabel Leventon. 'We were very excited about it because we felt that it was a break from tradition. The four-asterisk revue had been much in the mould of *Beyond the Fringe*, all based on social manners. *The Oxford Revue* was more fantastic. We did some very odd bits. We all sang a song about British nosh, and Michael had a song about having a long-range telescope. It got a terrific response. David Frost came round, but alas, we ended up with it in the Establishment Club, which had become very seedy by then. We often outnumbered the audience, which was strange because in Edinburgh we had played to packed houses and of course, the most famous number in it was the custard pie sketch which we gave to *Cambridge Circus*.

'I remember meeting John Cleese then. He really wasn't that much different. I remember having dinner with him in the Angus Steak House in Leicester Square and being very impressed by the amount of steak that he could put away. Michael White invited us to a party with the Cambridge lot. Anyway, that started off my first year out of Oxford.'

Rather than continuing to live at Claygate with his parents he rented a cheap room in Earls Court. Willie Donaldson gave him a small sum as an advance on the script of his proposed show about sex and for weeks Terry Jones leafed through library books seeking references on the history of lovemaking, with the intention of turning it into a musical in the style of *Hang Down Your Head and Die*. Michael Palin, a year behind him at Oxford, later joined in the stillborn project.

LEFT **Brian's mother, Mandy, in The Life of Brian**

43

'I had a Thai girlfriend who was still up at Oxford and she was giving me a rather hard time. I had a particularly bad phone call from her and felt I had to go up and see her or else see the end of the relationship, and at the time I was living in Lambeth and I remember walking across Lambeth Bridge and I got halfway over it and I thought "Sod it" – no, no, I wasn't thinking of committing suicide. I was overwhelmed by the symbolism of crossing bridges, and I thought, "This is no good, Oxford's a dead end and I'm not going to get anywhere." So I turned round and started phoning up people to get a job – it had not occurred to me before to try and get a job, and I nearly became a copywriter for Anglia Television. And then I suddenly got a phone call from Frank Muir's secretary asking me to go and meet him. He offered me a job at £20 a week at the BBC in Light Entertainment, to be a script editor officially, but to hang around and keep an eye on television and go to meetings and listen. I remember sitting in on discussions on *The Frost Report*, and whether they should go ahead with it or not, with people saying "Well, David Frost is a bit past it, isn't he?" It was a very interesting time – I had an office and a desk with four telephones on it. Occasionally I had stabs at writing sketches that never quite made it. But eventually I contributed a joke to Ken Dodd – it was the year Ken Dodd shot to the top – and in the Review of the Year they mentioned it with *my* joke, about a policeman's walking race.'

His career momentarily faltered when he was unable to finish a director's course

ABOVE **Jennifer Connelly and a goblin in *Labyrinth***

because he had peritonitis, but after a frustrating period as a production assistant he became attached to Rowan Ayres, the producer of a magazine programme called *Late Night Line-Up*. 'He took me on a as a jokesmith, and I wrote with Michael Palin, Barry Cryer and Robert Hewison. I didn't do the performing, they did. After that Mike and I began writing for *The Frost Report*, particularly visual jokes, our first taste of actual filming.'

While at the BBC he met his future wife Alison, newly graduated from Oxford and working as a technician in the Botany Department of the University of London. They married in 1970 and still live in the three-story Victorian house they had then, in Grove Park, on the heights south of Camberwell. At Oxford they never knew each other, although Alison recalls Terry and Michael performing a cabaret at her college, Lady Margaret Hall. She was sick during the performance and had to be escorted out. 'I do remember someone being ushered

out in the middle of one of my sketches,' says Terry, 'I didn't know it was my future wife and the mother of my children.' She has since pursued a career as a biochemist specializing in photosynthesis.

Their home is warm, friendly and alive. At the top of the house is Terry's spacious and bright work room, with an expansive view to the north across the rooftops to the high-rise office buildings of the City of London and the dome of St Paul's. The house has undergone many changes and improvements in the long time the Joneses have lived in it. 'We like it here. It seems to get better all the time – we have a real neighbourhood now in Grove Park.'

He remembers the Pythons coming together following his work on Humphrey Barclay's show for London Weekend, *Do Not Adjust Your Set*, with Michael Palin and Eric Idle, and other shows, *Broaden Your Mind* and *Marty* for the BBC, which involved Graham Chapman and John Cleese. 'In the last series of *Do Not Adjust Your Set* a chap named Terry Gilliam had been hanging around and had done a couple of animations. Eric was rather keen that he be involved. Michael and I meanwhile did a series for LWT, *The Complete and Utter History of Britain*. Then Barry Took suggested we all link up and do something for the BBC. I remember thinking at the time that there was no question it wasn't going to be the funniest show around, because John and Graham were writing wonderful material, and we thought we could write very funny material too, of a different kind. John and Graham were very verbal and we were a bit wackier and visual. I remember being very keen to get a distinctive format for the show. Then Spike Milligan had his series *Q5*. Suddenly I realized we had been writing cliches.'

LEFT **Michael Foreman and Terry: the team behind *Fantastic Stories*, *The Saga of Erik the Viking* and *Nicobobinus***

Various character portraits labelled around the poster:

VALLE THE MADDENINGLY CALM · FREYA SOOTHSAYER · HALFDAN THE BLACK · HARALD MISSIONARY · KING ARNULF THE UNMUSICAL · ERIK'S GRANDAD · A HORRIBLY SLAIN WARRIOR · A SLAVEDRIVER · LOKI THE UNMENTIONABLE · THORFINN SKULLSPLITTER · NJAL THE BONELESS · GRIMHILD HOUSEWIFE · PRINCESS AUD · SNORRI THE MISERABLE · HELGA · SVEN THE BERSERK · A DOGFIGHTER · KEITEL BLACKSMITH

'An adventure the end of the earth... and over it.'

ERIK the VIKING

ABOVE Poster for Erik the Viking, 1989

It was soon noted that he and Terry Gilliam were the most visually literate members of the team with a knowledge of film grammar. Initially he had to convince the *Python* director, Ian McNaughton, to allow him into the editing suite when the filmed inserts were being cut together, but once he had gained his confidence he was soon not only joining the pieces together himself, but supervising the shooting of them. The Pythons always grumbled that he was able to find the most rain-soaked, inhospitable locations in Britain, but for Terry Jones they had the virtue of not having been used to excess.

After the experience of *And Now for Something Completely Different* and interference from Victor Lownes, its producer, the Pythons were anxious to retain control of their next venture into film, *Monty Python and the Holy Grail* and the two Terrys were made co-directors. 'I really agree very easily about things. I especially did then. I enjoyed it, but I think Terry G found it a frustrating experience. The filming was a nightmare. Everybody was underpaid, including us, and doing it half for love. I felt badly about that because at least we had a percentage, whereas the technicians had no share. We had this loony schedule – scenes that should take a week were shot in a day.'

Its success did at least enable him to take a year off from show business and indulge in a passion that had been with him since schooldays, Chaucer. A book resulted, *Chaucer's Knight*, which looked at the character from *The Canterbury Tales* in its historical as well as literary context. He demonstrated that the Knight, far from being the gentle, chivalrous figure of traditional belief, was a hardened, callous mercenary. During the writing he amassed a wealth of rare texts on the period. He is in fact an avid collector where his enthusiasms are concerned. In making a Channel 4 documentary on another long-term interest, the children's character Rupert Bear, in the *Daily Express* since 1920, he tracked down its elderly, long-retired artist, Alfred Bestall in a remote cottage in Snowdonia and brought him back into the public eye in his twilight years. Terry Jones has a collection of the Rupert annuals, some of which are extremely rare and valuable. He is also a writer of original fairy stories, having composed his first to amuse his daughter Sally when she was a young child. *Fairy Tales* was published in 1981, followed by another collection in 1983, written this time for his son Bill, *The Saga of Erik the Viking*. A few years later he directed a film version with Tim Robbins in the lead role,

46

ABOVE **Terry Jones as the King in** *Erik the Viking*

and it was released in 1989. Other books included *Dr Fegg's Encyclopedia of All World Knowledge*, co-written with Michael Palin, and another children's story, *Nicobobinus*. A further book of children's yarns, *Fantastic Stories*, was published in 1992.

Terry wrote the screenplay of *Labyrinth* for Jim Henson, who later directed it, with Jennifer Connelly playing a teenage babysitter whose infant brother is kidnapped by the king of the goblins, played by David Bowie. In a completely different vein he directed *Personal Services* from a script by David Leland, a comedy based on the professional career of a celebrated South London brothel-keeper, Cynthia Payne, with Julie Walters as the madame who caters for a clientele consisting of well-behaved and discreet middle-class males. He also directed a story in the television series *Young Indiana Jones* for Lucasfilm. Currently among his many projects is a book and ambitious historical documentary series for BBC television on the Crusades, shot on locations in the Middle East. Simultaneously, with Brian Froud as artist, he launched *Lady Cottington's Pressed Fairy Book*, allegedly a facsimile of the late-Victorian diary by the woman who convinced Sir Arthur Conan Doyle that fairies existed.

Somehow in the midst of all his activity he has found time to produce a newspaper column for the *Guardian* and a collection of his articles was published in 1988 under the title *Attacks of Opinion*. His many hobby-horses include a concern for ecology and the environment, the ozone layer, the decline in social services, the concentration of media power, and the ethos of commercial greed that became unashamed during the 1980s. He fills his days with creative

RIGHT Tim Robbins and Imogen Stubbs in *Erik the Viking*

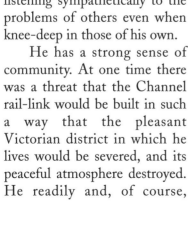

activity, and yet still finds time to talk to schools and local groups on his favourite subjects. By nature he admits to being a worrier, with a pessimistic view of what is being done to the planet, and he has the knack of listening sympathetically to the problems of others even when knee-deep in those of his own.

He has a strong sense of community. At one time there was a threat that the Channel rail-link would be built in such a way that the pleasant Victorian district in which he lives would be severed, and its peaceful atmosphere destroyed. He readily and, of course,

48

enthusiastically, took part in the protests, and the proposals were abandoned.

In Python politics Terry Jones is at the opposite end of the spectrum to John Cleese. Cleese's comedy is logical, ordered and brilliantly orchestrated. The apparent chaos of *Fawlty Towers* was the consequence of firm writing, careful blocking and precise timing. In contrast, Terry Jones is much more wild and anarchic, sometimes bizarre, and his humour often works through a sledgehammer effect. Their differences were essential to the success of *Monty Python* and Terry Jones, almost more than the others, was aware of the void when John dropped out of the fourth series, missing his scornful deflations in script meetings. The best programmes emerged from conflict, and without it bad ideas could be pushed through without encountering the challenge of argument. John was the first to develop a sense of independence from the Pythons, regarding it as perfectly possible to function successfully outside the group. Terry, on the other hand, is aware of the near-mystical importance of the Pythons as an entity, and more than any other of its members has kept its spirit alive. The difference of his perceptions is revealed by the final *Python* film *The Meaning of Life* in 1983, which was regarded by John as a virtually unmitigated nightmare of frustration, while Terry, its director, saw it as proceeding efficiently and smoothly, a dream compared with the earlier films. He is perhaps the Pythons' sheet anchor, and as long as he is around so are they.

LEFT **Julie Walters, John Shrapnel, Shirley Stelfox in *Personal Services*, 1986**

TERRY GILLIAM

The Pythons are all exceptional people, but none more so than Terry Gilliam. The reason is simple enough. They are British, he is American. He has lived long enough in London to be thoroughly anglicized should he so wish, but he retains his outsider's scepticism and wry amusement at the curious ways of the British, but would not want to live anywhere else. He stays closely in touch with the United States, too. His mother lives in Panorama City on the flat plain of the San Fernando Valley, and endured considerable inconvenience in the 1994 Los Angeles earthquake. His brother is a senior detective with the Los Angeles Police Department, having worked his way up from uniformed patrolman and a beat on Hollywood Boulevard among the transvestites, drug addicts and teenage hookers.

Terry Gilliam was not, however, born in California, but in Minnesota. His childhood was spent in the village of Medicine Lake, then a rural community a few miles west of Minneapolis, but now just another suburb within the orbit of Interstate 494, encircling the Twin Cities. A few years ago when I was on the committee of an annual seminar on visual communication at the University of Minnesota I suggested that he return to the city of his birth which he had last seen when he was eleven, and take part in the event. He happily made the journey, and took with him a print of his current film *Jabberwocky*, which he screened to a student audience assembled in the largest auditorium on the campus. He was anxious that the subsequent question-and-answer session would not require him to probe too deeply into the hidden meanings of the film, which he preferred to keep private, and with apprehension faced the first student interrogator. He need hardly have worried. A bespectacled arts major seized the hand microphone passing round the audience and said: 'Mr Gilliam, sir. Would you mind telling us where you got your shoes?'

Unerringly he had gone for a Gilliam obsession.

BORN 22ND NOVEMBER 1940

MEDICINE LAKE
MINNESOTA

TERRY GILLIAM

ABOVE **Sigma Alpha Epsilon house at Occidental
College, Los Angeles, 1960. Terry Gilliam is
sixth from left, front row**

Feet. The opening credits of the *Monty Python* shows conclude with a large foot crashing down from the top of the screen and crushing everything in its way. It is actually a Renaissance foot, lifted from a painting of Venus and Cupid by the Tuscan master, Bronzino, in London's National Gallery. The shoes that caught the attention of the Minnesota students were heavy-soled Kickers of a bilious shade of yellow and in the mid-1970s had probably never before been seen in the Middle West.

Terry Gilliam was born on 22 November 1940. His father had been a travelling salesman for Folger's Coffee, but quit to train as a carpenter. He came from Tennessee, had served in the last cavalry unit of the United States Army, and ended up in Minneapolis where he decided to stay as a civilian. Terry was the first-born, followed by a sister and brother, who is ten years younger than him. He remembers his rustic childhood: 'I never got living in the country out of my blood, it's something you can't get away from. The secret hideaways, the swamp, the moss-

BELOW Bemused Santa drawn by Terry Gilliam for his high school magazine

lined caves, treehouses. We had a little house on a dirt road, woods behind the house – it was a real Tom Sawyer, Huckleberry Finn upbringing. One of my earliest memories is running through the woods with a friend barefoot, and we went into a shack where a nail went through his foot and impaled him – I had to run home and get my father to pull it out.'

Winters in Minnesota were rugged. In the 1940s the Gilliams had no outside sanitation, which made answering the call of nature when the temperature was forty below freezing point an ordeal best not contemplated too closely. When indoor plumbing was eventually installed he converted the outside privy into a treehouse forty feet from the ground. He remembers his boyhood winter sport of jumping from it, safely into a deep snowdrift, after making an unsuccessful pass at high tension power lines on the way down.

In 1951 the Gilliams abandoned the snows of Minnesota for the sunshine of the Golden West. 'My sister was asthmatic and needed the drier air of California. My father, by then, was with Johns-Manville who were all over the States. The sad thing is that he was a very good carpenter, and he ended up making nothing else but office partitions.'

Terry went to Birmingham High School where he was able (he claims because of the abysmally low educational standards then prevailing in southern California) almost consistently to achieve straight As, and still earn the right to wear the school's letter on his jacket for pole-vaulting, be president of the student body, king of the senior prom and chosen as the pupil most likely to succeed. His appearance was that of a fearsome jock, with a crewcut of Marine Corps severity. On graduating from high school he moved on to Occidental College, working his way through with a number of jobs, including time on the assembly line of the

local Chevrolet plant. His drawing talent was developing and he discovered that he had a means for paying the rent literally at his fingertips. Having begun as a Physics major (he had a bent for science and mathematics) he switched after six weeks to Fine Arts only to find that the professor made the subject crushingly dull. He ended up majoring in Political Science, a course sufficiently fragmented to give him time to work on the college magazine.

'There was a group of us who became the campus clowns – it was before the word "happening" came into use, but that's what we were doing, trying to shock and entertain everyone else on campus.' Among the more baroque stunts was the concoction of a completely fictitious history of the institution and a repertoire of bogus traditional rituals which freshmen were required to learn

HeLP!

MAY 1965 • ICD • 35¢

DOWN
WITH
TOPLESS
BATHING SUITS!
LET US
DRESS
FOR THE
WATER.

LEFT **Gilliam poses for the cover of Harvey Kurtzman's humorous magazine, saving on model fees**

without being let in on the joke. Future generations were totally confused. He also joined a fraternity (Sigma Alpha Epsilon) but decided to participate only in the fun events, a privilege earned by designing their graphic material.

Terry Gilliam narrowly graduated from Occidental as a consequence of all his extra-curricular interests, although romantic entanglements were not on the agenda. 'I had incredibly high standards – I actually believed in love in those days. It had to be the right person, nothing less than the best, time which I didn't have. I left college as pure as the driven snow – it was quite awful.'

During the last year there he had sent samples of his cartooning in the college journal to Harvey Kurtzman in New York, who was then running a humour magazine called *Help!* After a favourable response he decided to move there and seek his fortune, although Kurtzman had warned him that work was hard to come by. A vacancy occurred on the editorial staff of *Help!* when Charles Alverson left, and Gilliam moved in. He was there for three years on a low

salary, discovering how to design page layouts. At that time he met John Cleese, who was onstage in New York in Cambridge Circus, and persuaded him to model for a photographic comic strip.

Then the draft loomed. Gilliam had enrolled in the National Guard to escape the full horror, but was nevertheless obliged to drop everything to report for basic training at Fort Dix, New Jersey where he remained for several months. He learned how to bypass the more unpleasant details by drawing flattering caricatures for the officers, and he also worked on the camp newspaper, a way of filling in the time. Army life required the art of looking busy without actually doing very much, and it was a trait he found difficult to be rid of when he returned to civilian life. He did not go back to the low pay of *Help!* having discovered that he was actually better off out-of-work and on welfare benefits. As good a time as any, Gilliam thought, to leave New York and take a look at Europe. He hitched around the continent, and bought a secondhand motorcycle which was so unreliable that he eventually hurled it from a Spanish cliff. When his money ran out he worked temporarily in Paris for René Goscinny on *Pilote* magazine. 'Being a cartoonist is the next best thing to being a musician. Just as it doesn't matter about language if you can strum a guitar, it's the same with cartooning if you get into a tight spot.'

He returned to New York, lived for a time in Harvey Kurtzman's attic while he decided whether or not to stay in America, then went west to Los Angeles, where he worked first as a freelance illustrator and then in an advertising agency. Becoming dissatisfied with office life Gilliam stopped taking it seriously, and eventually decided to resign, but before he was able to send in his letter he was fired. At that time he was living with a British journalist, Glenys Roberts, who was in Los Angeles trying to recover from a broken marriage. She persuaded him that London would be more appreciative of his talents. Gilliam decided to

take her advice and go there. Although he found a number of outlets for his work including the innovative *Sunday Times Magazine*, it was hard to make an adequate living. His morale sank to zero when he worked on *The Londoner*, a publication modelled on the formula of the successful *New York* magazine, which quickly collapsed.

'It seemed impossible to get anywhere with magazines, so I called John Cleese and asked him how I could get into television. He suggested contacting Humphrey Barclay, and eventually I got to him. He was only mildly amused by my written sketches, but when I mentioned that I was a cartoonist he was interested. It helped that Humphrey was a cartoonist. Somehow he found room for one or two things I had written in *Do Not Adjust Your Set*, which did not endear me to Michael Palin or Terry Jones. Eric Idle was the nice one – he took me under his wing. Eric is very good with new people. Then Humphrey went over to London Weekend when they started up. We did a wonderful show with Frank Muir and when we got through it we were told that no one saw it because there had been a dispute and the whole thing was blacked – it wasn't even videotaped. But it led to *Monty Python*.

'I knew the techniques of animation in theory, having read a book or two, but I had never done anything in practice. The cutout technique I had seen years earlier in New York. It was

BELOW **Max Wall as Bruno the Questionable on the throne, Michael Palin in front on him and other cast members of *Jabberwocky***

fast and crude. If I had been given the money and time I would probably have tried to do a Walt Disney style. I think I was good with sound effects and the timing. The noises are fifty per cent of the effect.'

He was spared the ritual ordeal of reading his material to the other Pythons during the weekly script sessions. His contributions were mainly the animated graphics and link sequences which would seem surreal even in a *Monty Python* context. Only occasionally did he play characters, such as Cardinal Fang in the Spanish Inquisition team.

'I have never developed the presentation skills the others have had to develop. They got better and better, because

ABOVE *Time Bandits*
with David Rappaport,
left, Ian Holm as
Napoleon

RIGHT Poster for Terry
Gilliam's *Time Bandits*, 1981

56

before they could present their stuff to the audience they first had to present it to the group, which was very demanding. The only skill I had was to be able to do it, and ultimately let the result speak for itself. I didn't have to sell it. But even people like Terry Jones and Mike who were the most sympathetic – when I'd tell them over the phone what I was doing there would be these embarrassed silences. It would be necessary for me to produce the finished article before they would know what I was talking about.'

There was also a practical argument for avoiding such presentations. Time was always short, and discussion could hold up the work, affecting the taping of the programme. A tight deadline could, he discovered, be used to advantage as a sure way of getting his work through without being questioned.

'I'd literally work day and night when we were doing a series. The BBC had an excellent rostrum camera set-up. I'd be going seven days a week, usually with two all-nighters, churning out artwork, then I'd go down there to play with it under a camera.'

Within the Python political spectrum he sided with the Oxford graduates, Terry Jones and Michael Palin. 'We were the workhorses, the sloggers, the guys who really sweated it out to get it right. We were the ones who stayed up all night in the cutting room. John and Graham and Eric came in and did what they had to do and did it brilliantly, then walked away from it. It's true that the Oxford men are the romantics, the Cambridge ones the pragmatists.

BELOW **A Terry Gilliam
foot makes an imprint
in *Time Bandits***

They're really ruthless. They know just what they want.' As the only non-Oxbridge member of the team and an American he found himself in the best position to appreciate the differences in temperament, and to realize that the polarities and differences were essential, generating an abrasive interaction that brought about their spiky, surreal and unsettling brand of humour.

Terry Gilliam believes that the choice of John Philip Sousa's march *Liberty Bell*, as the *Python* introductory theme also arose during these creative sessions. He suspects that it was Roger Last, the programme production assistant, who suggested it when they were trying to find a recording that suited the mood of the animated titles. Alas, no one now knows for sure exactly how it happened.

Indisputably, Gilliam imposed a particular visual style on all the *Python* graphics that was to extend to books, record

57

album sleeves, films, stage shows, tee-shirts and other memorabilia. Following the bad experience of making *And Now for Something Completely Different*, the Pythons took control of their own work and it was regarded as appropriate that henceforth the two Terrys, Gilliam and Jones, both deeply interested in film-making and editing, would direct. The first result was *Monty Python and the Holy Grail*. The directing partnership produced a successful film in spite of budgetary and logistical difficulties, but Gilliam found the experience less satisfactory than Jones, and when the time came to make *The Life of Brian* he let the latter have the directing to himself. Meanwhile he had made *Jabberwocky* from a screenplay co-written with Charles Alverson, an old friend, with Michael Palin playing the leading character. Gilliam was at pains to ensure that it was not regarded as a *Python* film, although the American distributors played up the connection in its promotion. It achieved only modest results at the box office, audiences finding the emphasis on dirt and gore disturbing. Gilliam had wanted to distance himself from the conventions of Hollywood costume films in which everyone looks bandbox fresh, but had gone too far in allowing his hero to pick his way through mountains of filth and ordure.

Gilliam's next film, *Time Bandits*, was altogether more satisfactory, in spite of a few carping London reviews. He had wanted to make an adventure that would have some appeal for children, and made his hero a small boy called Kevin, who is taken by a gang of marauding, picaresque dwarfs on a series of time trips encountering such characters as Napoleon (Ian Holm), Robin Hood (John Cleese) and Agamemnon (Sean Connery.) The action is resolved in a battle between Good, represented by Sir Ralph Richardson, and Evil, David Warner. Kevin and the dwarfs get on because they are of the same height. It proved very popular with children, who were more able than some adults to accept the sudden changes of pace and scene as the adventurers flipped through the temporal dimension.

In the United States *Time Bandits* was a huge success, bringing in much-needed revenue for HandMade Films – the company formed by George Harrison and Denis O'Brien which had backed the project – and it greatly boosted the financial attractiveness of finance for the next *Python* movie proper. When *The Meaning of Life* was nearing production it was decided that while Terry Jones would direct the main part of the film, Terry Gilliam would be in charge of a special section, known as 'the other unit.' Gilliam,

BELOW **Michael Palin and Shelley Duvall in *Time Bandits***

able to utilize his biggest budget to date, devised a sequence in which a staid City insurance company peopled by elderly clerks using antique office equipment suddenly turns on its new employers, the young whizkids in a multi-national conglomerate. Using the materials to hand, filing cabinets as cannon, fan blades as cutlasses, hat racks as grappling hooks, they mount a piratical and successful onslaught, and having triumphed, uproot the anchor that ties their Edwardian building firmly to its surroundings and sail off along city streets to the strains of bogus Korngold music reminiscent of *The Sea Hawk*. The intention had been to make the sequence an interlude in the middle of the film, but previews were unfavourable – it seemed to halt the main flow rather too forcefully – so it was decided to place it at the beginning as a detached prologue.

Following *The Meaning of Life* Gilliam embarked on a hugely ambitious film of his own

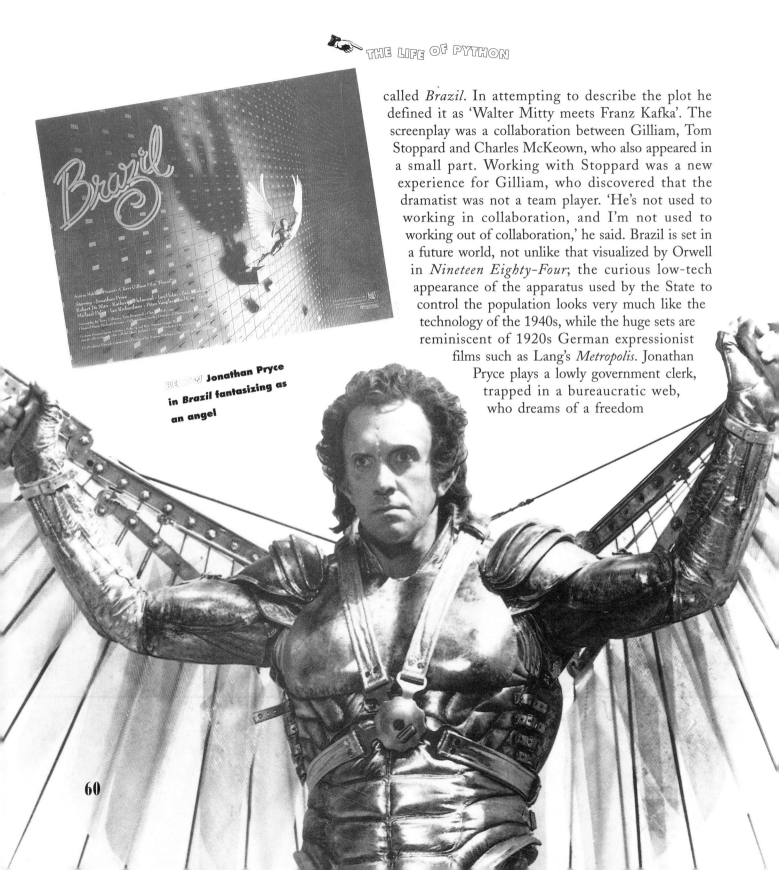

called *Brazil*. In attempting to describe the plot he defined it as 'Walter Mitty meets Franz Kafka'. The screenplay was a collaboration between Gilliam, Tom Stoppard and Charles McKeown, who also appeared in a small part. Working with Stoppard was a new experience for Gilliam, who discovered that the dramatist was not a team player. 'He's not used to working in collaboration, and I'm not used to working out of collaboration,' he said. Brazil is set in a future world, not unlike that visualized by Orwell in *Nineteen Eighty-Four*; the curious low-tech appearance of the apparatus used by the State to control the population looks very much like the technology of the 1940s, while the huge sets are reminiscent of 1920s German expressionist films such as Lang's *Metropolis*. Jonathan Pryce plays a lowly government clerk, trapped in a bureaucratic web, who dreams of a freedom

60

far away in the company of a beautiful girl, played by Kim Greist. One of the film's most effective performances is that of Robert De Niro in a small role, playing a kind of guerilla heating engineer. Michael Palin for once was cast against type, as a particularly nasty government torturer. *Brazil*, the title taken from a frivolous popular song and intended to signify escapist yearnings, is black and bleak, but also very funny, and some of the images have an extraordinary power.

Gilliam had to struggle hard to make his film. It had been in gestation for years and raising the money was difficult. When it was finally finished there were still problems over its release. Twentieth Century Fox were responsible for distribution in most territories, but not the United States where Universal put *Brazil* on the shelf on the grounds that it was too long. Gilliam re-edited, and submitted a 130-minute version, but they were still concerned that the ending was too pessimistic. The film concludes with what appears to be a happy ending, from which the rug is suddenly and brutally pulled, and the irony was essential to the film's concept. Universal disagreed. Eventually Gilliam took out a full-page advertisement in *Variety*: 'Dear Sid Sheinberg – when are you going to release *Brazil*? Terry Gilliam.'

Screenings to journalists and at the Deauville Film Festival were well received, but to no avail. When *Brazil* was finally released in America it went largely unsupported by promotion and was a failure at the box office. Later, Universal released its own edited version for television which Gilliam completely disowned. His original film, which has been shown by BBC television, remains a milestone of imaginative cinema.

BELOW **Robert De Niro in *Brazil* as a guerilla and freelance heating engineer**

The *Brazil* saga was insignificant compared with the debacle on his next film, *The Adventures of Baron Munchausen*. He had been drawn to the idea for years, and saw it as the final instalment of a trilogy beginning with *Time Bandits* in which a boy travels through space and time with no knowledge of what is real and what is dream and *Brazil* in which a man dreams his way out of reality. *Munchausen* is the story of a classic liar, a cavalry officer in Frederick the Great's army who in later life became renowned for his tall stories – his journey to the moon, his sojourn in a sea monster's belly, his ride through the air on a cannon ball. With Charles McKeown as co-writer Gilliam concocted a story in which a group of actors in an

eighteenth-century town under siege from the Turks is putting on a stage performance based on Munchausen's adventures when the real baron (played by John Neville) interrupts, and stages an elaborate escape from the besiegers in a hot-air balloon made from women's drawers. 'A nightmare,' said Gilliam. 'There had to be a real balloon inside all that underwear. We found that it wouldn't go up if the wind was blowing at more than a couple of knots. The money had run out and they were trying to close the film. I said foolishly if the balloon flies we'll finish it. But the weather stayed bad. Then with only an hour to go we got it up, but it went the wrong way. Finally the sun broke through and we got the perfect shot.'

ABOVE **Terry Gilliam on the set of *The Adventures of Baron Munchausen***

Shot on location in Spain and Italy with studio work at CineCittà in Rome and special effects in Britain, it was a financial disaster. Gilliam unjustly took the blame for the hugely overspent budget, which was in fact the responsibility of its German producer, Thomas Schüly who on arrival in Rome had unwisely announced that it was to be the biggest production there since Taylor and Burton's *Cleopatra* (perhaps proportionately the costliest film ever made). The Italian suppliers trebled their prices accordingly.

Gilliam's fellow Python, Eric Idle was in the cast, playing Berthold, the fastest runner in the world. While waiting for a scene in which he was to be forcibly ducked in the studio tank he said: 'Filming is hours of interminable waiting punctuated by short periods of indescribable discomfort.' Robin Williams took the role of the Moon King, appearing as a detached head. 'We had a gimbal mechanism into which he was strapped and swung around the set,' said Gilliam. 'Even though he had just come off a plane from the States he didn't seem to mind, it didn't stop him from being brilliant with his ad libs. I always think there is a streak of masochism in actors.'

Its release occurred shortly after the departure of David Puttnam as head of production at Columbia, a difficult time in the studio's history. A campaign against Puttnam had been waged, embracing the films made under his aegis, and although *Munchausen* was not one, it was perceived to be. Very little money was spent on promotion and only one hundred and fifteen prints were struck (a full US release can require two-and-a-half thousand).

Exhausted from the experiences of *Brazil* and *Munchausen* Gilliam pursued a different

LEFT **Poster for Munchausen, a troubled production, made in Rome**

BELOW **Escaping the siege in a hot-air balloon made from women's underwear**

ABOVE **Gilliam in New York directing** *The Fisher King*, **with Robin Williams**

course for his next film, picking up a screenplay that was not his, but had been written by Richard Lagravenese. In *The Fisher King*, a modern fairy tale, Jeff Bridges plays Jack Lucas, an acerbic disc jockey in New York whose ill-considered remarks prompt a caller to go off and shoot people at random in a crowded New York bar. Feelings of guilt destroy his career and three years later, having sunk into alcoholic depression, he is rescued from suicide by Parry, a crazed down-and-out, played by Robin Williams, whose speech drifts into Arthurian gibberish and who seems to believe that the Holy Grail is located in a billionaire's Fifth Avenue mansion. Events reveal that the Williams character was formerly a quiet academic who had been dining out with his wife when the maniac had burst into the restaurant, and she was one of his victims. Jack can find redemption, first by retrieving the Grail from the castellated mansion and second, by uniting his rescuer with a lonely girl (Amanda Plummer) on whom he has become fixated. The film lacks the customary Gilliam special effects, other than a spectral red knight on horseback who haunts Parry by riding through the New York streets, but the most spectacular bravura sequence occurs when homebound commuters crossing the handsome concourse of Grand Central Station suddenly become couples waltzing in an enchanted ballroom, then resume their homeward path as though nothing strange has happened.

It was not an easy work to shoot (the Grand Central sequence was filmed with a thousand extras through the short night between the last and first trains) but was the most commercially successful of Gilliam's movies, a total vindication after *Munchausen*, and received four Academy Award nominations. Mercedes Ruehl, who played Jeff Bridges' girlfriend, won an Oscar for her performance. It was also voted best film at the Toronto Film Festival and Robin Williams collected a Golden Globe. In one sense it is not a true Gilliam film, with its inherited screenplay and romantic style, but there are occasional glimpses of Gilliam's imagination working its magic. He has since been writing another screenplay with Richard Lagravense called *The Defective Detective*, and also has plans eventually to make the first definitive screen

64

version of Mark Twain's *A Connecticut Yankee*. 'It's a much darker satire than anyone believes. They always think that it's Bing Crosby fooling around in King Arthur's time.' He works constantly to get the next project off the ground. The film industry is tough, and the most successful directors spend ninety per cent of their time endeavouring to raise backing for the next film.

In 1973 he married Maggie Weston, the make-up girl on the *Python* shows, who has continued a career in her own right, with encouragement from Terry. The Gilliams have three children, Harry, Amy and Holly and live in a fine seventeenth-century house on the Highgate heights.

LEFT *The Fisher King* is Gilliam's most successful film, critically and financially

Having lived in Britain since the 1960s Terry Gilliam has become almost totally assimilated and has no desire to make a permanent return to the land of his birth, although he visits frequently, and directed *The Fisher King* there. Hollywood holds little excitement – it represents exasperation and a peculiar kind of small-mindedness particular to the film industry. Now that he is in his fifties his twitchy creative restlessness is more subdued, and the frustrations he has suffered have had their effect. He still works immensely hard, and still stares out of the window. In his *Debrett's People of Today* entry he gives his recreation as sitting extremely still for indeterminate amounts of time. Charles Alverson, who has known him longer than anyone else in Britain, but fell out over a project that went wrong, once predicted that the Gilliam ambition would eventually mess him up, especially if it drove him back to America to make his films. So far it has not happened, but there has been a distancing from other members of the Pythons, largely because his special talents are resistant to homogenization. He can be extremely critical of their endeavours in that candid, open manner of the group.

ABOVE Gilliam with Jeff Bridges, his star in *The Fisher King*, 1991

Terry Gilliam has had a bumpy career as a film-maker, with *The Adventures of Baron Munchausen* having the distinction of being one of the most costly flops in film history, but nevertheless can be regarded as one of the cinema's most original voices. That he has been responsible for as much originality as he has within the mainstream commercial framework is a considerable achievement in itself in an industry that always tries to categorize its talent. Gilliam is determined not to be pigeon-holed or substituted, and would be unable to function in any other way. His best work may yet be to come.

JOHN CLEESE

Having now reached his mid-fifties and his third American wife, John Cleese has mellowed. Why, it has to be asked, does he always marry Americans? 'It's my answer to the English class system,' he observes, 'I don't have to make my mind up about it.'

The mellowing process has taken several years. In the days of *Monty Python's Flying Circus* the others saw him as the most abrasively stubborn of their number, in a group that was not renowned for its capacity for mutual agreement. Cleese actually departed altogether from the fourth series, the only Python not to have seen through every one of the shows. He is extremely honest about the grumbling aspect of his character and in the late 1970s embarked on an intense course of psychotherapy, including group sessions, with Robin Skynner. The effect on his outlook was so dramatic that it prompted him to co-author a book with Skynner enabling others to benefit from the process of self-awareness. 'A lot of the ideas were then very new and there didn't seem to be any other place where you could find them, except in a rather feeble and diluted form in *Cosmopolitan*. I suggested to Robin that we should make some television programmes, but we found that no one in television is interested in ideas, they're only interested in whether it's going to make nice pictures. So we decided to go for book form.'

In ten years *Families and How to Survive Them* has become an extraordinary bestseller, having maintained a steady average sale of four hundred books a week. 'We did a radio series and it went up and is now selling at the rate of five hundred, but it is not on the bestseller list for only one reason – it is divided into two editions. It's been kind of accepted as a classic. It even got a good review in the *Sun*.

BORN 27TH OCTOBER 1939

WESTON-SUPER-MARE
SOMERSET

RIGHT **John Cleese: prickliest of the Pythons, the only one to quit a series**

JOHN CLEESE

ABOVE **At Cambridge Cleese measures his height against a crossing beacon**

BELOW **Clowning for the Footlights, in Cambridge Circus, 1963**

When was the last time you even saw a book review in the *Sun*? They wanted to quote some of the things I said about my sex life, and the way they did it was by taking extracts, and putting a couple of paragraphs around it to make it into a review.'

In 1993 he and Robin Skynner brought out a sequel, *Life and How to Survive It*, which has also been a remarkable publishing success. The year before he had married Alyce Faye Eichelberger, a psychologist from Texas whose experience includes a period working with children at the Tavistock Institute in London. She is very definitely not of the world of show business, and is even unfamiliar with much of the *Python* phenomenon, which passed her by unnoticed.

John Marwood Cleese was born on 27 October 1939 in Weston-super-Mare, then a seaside resort in Somerset, but since relocated in the upstart county of Avon, which has had the effect of turning the place into a Bristol outer suburb. His parents were both in their forties when he was born. His father, an insurance salesman, had changed his name from Cheese on joining the army during the First World War. They made strenuous efforts and sacrifices to enable their son to have a private education, initially at St Peter's Preparatory School in Weston, then at Clifton College where he was a day boy. He was aware there of an unspoken prejudice emanating from the boarders who regarded day boys as inferior.

BELOW **With his first wife, Connie Booth as they write** *Fawlty Towers*

'I was always something of an outsider. I was immensely tall. I was six feet at twelve and by the time I got to Clifton I remember being measured for my Corps uniforms, I suppose in my second term, and I was 6'4" then. I was astounded that I was so tall. I haven't grown upwards since. I've just put on about six stone.

'The problem with being tall was that it was always hard to fade into the background. I remember a master making a joke about me being a prominent citizen and I thought it was a compliment, and then he got a laugh out of the form by saying that he meant that I stuck out a lot. I always had this outsider status, which I think has gone on for years. It's a bit like my relationship with show business – I don't feel that I'm one hundred per cent in it. I was an immensely meek boy

and I was bullied a lot. I remember my father coming down to watch me play in a football match and finding three people sitting on me. I had a lot of problems at asserting normal healthy aggression. I think that went on for a long time; even at Clifton when I was playing soccer I didn't like the violent side of it, and if someone kicked me, almost on a point of principle, I wouldn't kick them back. It's taken me many years to get any confidence in that sort of self-assertive behaviour – like most English people I do not like scenes or rows.'

When he was at Clifton the fees were a mere sixty pounds a term and because he was good at mathematics he was able to win a scholarship worth thirty-six pounds per annum which reduced his father's outlay by a fifth. He was placed in a scholarship form where he was

ABOVE **The staff of *Fawlty Towers*: John Cleese (Basil), Connie Booth (Polly), Prunella Scales (Sybil), Andrew Sachs (Manuel)**

69

RIGHT Basil terrorizes Manuel in a *Fawlty Towers* episode

LEFT Disposing of a guest inconsiderate enough to die while staying there

RIGHT Another culinary catastrophe in the *Fawlty Towers* kitchen

found to be excellent at English and Latin. 'I always performed well in exams, I think because I was reasonably organized and a bit cynical about them, I saw what they were about. I didn't have any illusions, so I went for them in a cold-blooded way and got good results.

'Nobody in my family had ever been near a university, but my father, who was an immensely kind man, let me stick to my intention, and somehow found the money for a final year at the school during which I sat the entrance exam for Downing College, Cambridge. I had to wait two years before I could go, as they had just abolished National Service and were deluged with people. Instead of getting out of the country to go away and learn a language, I was so unenterprising I retired away to Weston-super-Mare, to teach at my old prep school and I went up to Cambridge at twenty-one.'

LEFT Basil muffles a complaining diner

Although his A-levels were in Maths, Physics and Chemistry he decided to read Law. 'I was never going to compete with the scientists at Cambridge who were highly-motivated. Science for me was something I had been put into because I was a reasonable mathematician. So I looked around for what I could escape into. There was a family tradition of law, which I took quite seriously. I didn't really examine it until I found out it meant that my grandfather had been a solicitor's clerk.

'I never had any ambition to be a barrister, that was a bit up-market for me. I think I could have done it pretty well, actually. My strength is in argument, because I've got a good line in logic, and a very good line in dismounting bad arguments. I think I'm most amusing when I'm ridiculing other people's arguments – I don't think of myself as amusing ordinarily, but if I'm in an argument with someone I'm quite good at touching the weak points. Barristers work so hard. They're the most compulsive workers of the lot. They flog themselves. They're strange creatures because they get so transported into the realm of words that they tend more than any other profession I've come across to lose contact with their feelings. It was very revealing that barristers turned up most in group therapy – more lawyers than anyone else.'

At school he had written, produced and appeared in a number of house entertainments, which were as daringly subversive as it was possible to be at an English public school in the 1950s. At Cambridge he attempted to join the Footlights. He found it harder than expected. He was asked if he sang or danced and confessed to being non-proficient at both. He was then asked if there was anything he could do and he answered 'I try to make people laugh'. Having made his statement, which he felt sounded pathetically lame, he rushed away and did not go near the Footlights for the next two terms.

BELOW **Tall Cleese looks down on short Ronnie Corbett in a** *Video Arts* **short**

'Then my closest friend, a guy called Alan Hutchison who is now a publisher, bumped into the Treasurer who asked him to do something, so he mentioned me, and was told we should try to write together. We sat down and produced three pieces – one of which was pinched from the funny columnist, Peter Simple, in the *Daily Telegraph* (a send-up of Montgomery) and one of which was pinched from a radio show, and one of which was a send-up of a news item. We went along and auditioned them and people seemed very friendly. Then we did them in front of an audience and we were elected. But then I wrote some other pieces and they were so terrible I wasn't allowed to perform them. Their revue that year was called *I Thought I Saw It Move* which David Frost was in, and I auditioned for it, but there wasn't any hope. But the funny thing was that when we came back the next term we wandered into the Footlights club room after about the second day, and found that we were on the committee because everyone else had left. Suddenly we were the big boys.

'What was so wonderful about the Footlights was that it was there and it had to be done. Whereas in Oxford they had to start from scratch and organize everything. Of course all the people who are good at doing jokes and sketches are terrible at hiring lights. Humphrey Barclay was the only guy I've ever known who was good at both.

'I've always felt, speaking for my generation, that Cambridge people were more efficient. Oxford people tend to be woollier. Even to the way they dress. Michael Palin always wears softer kinds of clothes. They are often much less clear in their objectives. At Cambridge most

groups, the politicians, the journalists and straight actors were very aware of London, and knew where they were going. Mind you, I don't think it was true of the Footlights in my year – I don't think there was a single one of them who really seriously contemplated going into show business.

'I nearly didn't do *A Clump of Plinths*, the Footlights show that became *Cambridge Circus*. I fell in love, an extraordinary new experience and I couldn't cope with it at all. I couldn't get any work done, and halfway through my second term in my last year I decided more or less not to do the revue because it didn't seem to matter. After all, I'd done it the year before when Trevor Nunn was directing. Then I remember thinking one weekend that I rather liked the blokes, and that it would only be two weeks in Cambridge and we'd be finished, so I did it. I realized it was pretty good, but didn't think it was all that special, and after about four days I went into the club room, and there were these two guys in grey suits, Peter Titheradge and Ted Taylor, and I suddenly realized they were asking if I wanted a job at the BBC. Then I discovered they'd offered one to Humphrey and to Bill (Oddie) – they were going for people who could be producers or writers. I was supposed to be joining a firm of solicitors in the City called Freshfields, at twelve pounds a week, and here they were offering thirty pounds. I thought, why not? So I went with them. And then *Cambridge Circus* was signed for the West End. Suddenly we were young people who were successful and were having newspaper articles written about us.'

He found it hard to resist the opportunity to tour New Zealand when the West End run concluded, and he obtained leave from the BBC. The thought of an antipodean trip which extended the life of the show seemed to offer the prospect of adventure, although the reality proved rather less exciting.

'New Zealand was a hopelessly inefficient place. It's all to do with standards. If you don't know what's good you can't provide it. I

LEFT **John Cleese disguised as Queen Elizabeth I in** *Decisions, Decisions,* **a** *Video Arts* **film**

BELOW **Cleese doing a Monty, General Montgomery, that is**

remember Johnny Lynn and I going into the opening of a new restaurant in Christchurch. It was freezing. Johnny ordered a bottle of red wine, and it was brought to the table stone cold. Johnny said that at least it was room temperature.'

After New Zealand the company progressed to Broadway, spending three days back in England *en route*. 'I was far more interested in being in New York than doing the show. We were falsely confident about it, and none of us appreciated the cultural gap. As we rehearsed we realized that the people who had invited us didn't know the first thing about our work, and there was a crisis. We were killed by the total lack of publicity and the fact that the *New York Times* sent a sports writer to review it. By the time Walter Kerr did his fantastic piece we had closed.'

At around the same time Terry Gilliam, then working for Harvey Kurtzman's humour magazine *Help!*, approached Cleese and asked him to participate in his photographed comic strip in which a middle-class suburbanite becomes enamoured of a Barbie doll. 'I liked Terry enormously,' said Cleese, 'and I think that he thought that I was good at mugging, which is supposed to be a sort of compliment.'

When *Cambridge Circus* had exhausted itself in its final brief run in the Village he decided to stay for a while in New York. In spite of his remarkable inability to sing, he was asked to audition for a part in the Broadway production of *Half a Sixpence*, starring Tommy Steele, and much to his surprise he got it. He was paid what seemed like an astronomical sum, two hundred dollars a week, and enjoyed the experience greatly even though the director who hired him was replaced by Gene Saks, who was far less sympathetic.

His next career move seemed to be even more miscast. On a subway platform he had found himself chatting to a man who turned out to be a journalist working for *Newsweek* magazine. Cleese expressed a certain wistful enviousness for the comforts and pleasures of a journalist's life, and an introduction was arranged to the international editor, who to his surprise offered him a job. His sponsor then went on a protracted foreign assignment and Cleese found that he was having to work in an unfamiliar office without training. He realized that he was doomed when he was appointed to the task of compiling obituaries of people who were not yet dead, and he quit before he was fired. At the end of 1965 he returned to England to contribute to *The Frost Report*.

In New York he had met a young actress who was spending more time waiting tables than performing, a common enough plight. The courtship of John Cleese and Connie Booth was a long one. She was unwilling to uproot and settle in a new country when he returned to England and their affair was conducted across the Atlantic. Meetings were restricted to twice a year until the start of 1968 when, having become established in British television, he suggested they married. They settled in a modern town house in Woodsford Square, surrounded by the palatial Victorian villas of Holland Park, two of which (joined together) he now lives in, and in 1971 their daughter Cynthia was born. By then *Monty Python* was taking up ten months of his year and he was beginning to resent the time devoted to it. 'I had enjoyed the first series enormously, but I felt that it was like being married to *Python*. I was feeling very constricted and I wanted to get away. They all felt I was being disloyal when I quit.'

The fourth series took place without him. Meanwhile with Connie he began work on a situation comedy built around an appalling hotelier the Pythons had encountered during one of their location excursions. *Fawlty Towers* turned out to be a high-water mark in television comedy. Cleese played the dreadful Basil Fawlty whose capacity to be a target for calamity was exacerbated by his short-fused temper and tendency to become hysterical. Countering him was Sybil, his infuriatingly calm and capable wife with a talent for making any chaotic situation much worse, another masterly comic creation played with great skill by Prunella Scales. Manuel, a dim Spanish waiter with a tenuous grip on the English language and the constant butt of Basil's ill humour, was played by Andrew Sachs. Connie Booth not only co-wrote the two series, but also took the role of Polly, the ever-willing but ineffective helper. Only twelve programmes were produced, leaving no opportunities for the idea to become over-extended.

BELOW Cleese as the knuckle-headed major in *Privates on Parade*

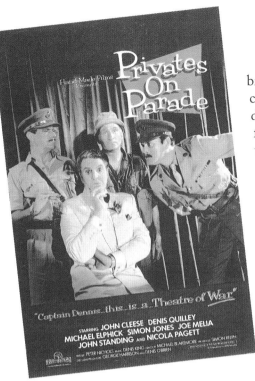

Ironically, while the writing partnership was proceeding brilliantly the marriage was not, and after several off-on crises the decision to end it was taken in 1976. 'Having done the psychotherapy, we don't think in terms of whose fault it was. It was very much a fifty-fifty thing. We stayed very good friends.'

In 1981 he married Barbara Trentham, an American TV film director he had met in Los Angeles when he was appearing in *Monty Python Live at the Hollywood Bowl*. 'I'd always assumed that I would get married again because I think that it is the ideal state. I like it.' In 1984 their daughter Camilla was born. But in 1990 the second marriage also came to an end.

'Cyn is now in her third year at UCLA as a drama major. She has a great natural talent. Camilla is living in Chicago with Babs. I'm perfectly happy to say that now I'm married to Alyce, she was prescribed by my doctor. Johnny Gaynor, a great friend of mine whose marriage had just broken up, invited me to dinner. I arrived and there were three chairs. Alyce Faye Eichelberger walked in thinking it was a dinner for twelve. She then hit on me to give money to her child psychotherapy trust. We lived together for the next year and got married at the end of 1992. It is a happy relationship that works – quite marvellous – it has changed the tone of my life. She was married to a pro golfer, Dave Eichelberger, and spent ten years going round on tours, playing bridge with Jack Nicklaus and so on. When the relationship broke up she came here to train at the Tavvy as a child psychoanalyst. She has two sons, Martin who is twenty-four and Clinton, the younger one. I remember a dinner when John Mortimer's eyes nearly popped out when she said she was going to help Clinton because he was having a few problems with girls.

'Americans have an energy that I like. There is a greater immediate warmth from them. Insanity in the UK and the US is different. They have shrinks for animals, allergies and food fads and cults. We have train spotters. We are all just as mad but different. Most of the people I like have been Americans who have spent time in Europe, or Europeans who have spent time in America. I feel the British are too sceptical – a bit too can't-do – their humour relies on irony and funny voices. The Americans perhaps are too can-do and can be naive and lacking in irony. But put the two together and the balance is right. The thing about any culture is that there are bound to be bits of it that are good and bad. If I'm on the West coast in jeans, tennis shoes and white shirt I can have as good a time there as I can

LEFT The cast of *Privates on Parade*

LEFT Cleese was annoyed when a trailer put too much emphasis on his silly walks

here. Some of the most interesting people intellectually are in northern California. I know four people there who I would probably like to talk to more than almost anyone else.'

For someone who once claimed that film acting was about as interesting as waiting for a flight at Heathrow for six weeks, he has still managed to dedicate much of his career to the cinema. There are of course the *Python* films, and those such as *Time Bandits* and *Yellowbeard* which were the consequence of initiatives by his fellow-Pythons. In 1982 he played a singularly stupid British army officer in the film version of Peter Nichols' play *Privates on Parade*, directed by Michael Blakemore, and it was his first full screen role. He was annoyed that a television trailer for it made much of the silly walks he had performed after the end titles, which he felt gave a misleading impression of his performance, as though it was a *Python* extension.

The *Python* reputation receded much further when he appeared in the engaging western *Silverado*, which was written and directed by Lawrence Kasdan, and shot on location in New Mexico. He played a straight-backed English sheriff, which was not totally implausible in the Old West, and had to take riding lessons for the role. It was followed back in Britain by *Clockwise*, directed by Christopher Morahan, and written by another comedy playwright whom he greatly admires, Michael Frayn. John Cleese played the head of a comprehensive school whose ego is unexpectedly boosted when he is invited to address the Headmasters' Conference, an elite gathering normally confined to the independent sector of education. Unfortunately he catches the wrong train, and then spends the day trying to get to Norwich and the conference centre in spite of an increasingly desperate series of misfortunes.

'I like a lot of the early part of the film enormously, but I think we screwed up the ending. We were trying to tell too many stories. We should have been cruder, we should have let

BELOW **Tall in the saddle as Sheriff Langston in Lawrence Kasdan's *Silverado*, 1985, with Todd Allen as his deputy**

Stimson [John Cleese's character] win the headmasters over, because he has them on the run when he treats them like school kids. The ending is a downer. We were all wrong, Christopher Morahan, Michael Frayn and I, we should have spotted that we were torpedoing a good film.'

A knee injury on the eve of shooting made much of it a painful experience, and permanently curtailed both his silly walks and his off-duty games of squash and cricket. 'I was limping like a cripple for most of the movie. I just about managed to hide it. You don't really see it except if you watch very carefully on the railway station, which was shot the day after.'

In association with Charles Crichton, the veteran director of the classic Ealing comedies *Hue and Cry*, *The Lavender Hill Mob* and *The Titfield Thunderbolt*, which were made between 1947 and 1953, Cleese wrote the script for a new comedy of the 1980s. Crichton (born in 1910) made a masterly return to his métier, directing *A Fish Called Wanda*, which reached the number one position in the US box-office chart to become the most successful British comedy ever shown there. Part of its appeal lay in the cunning interweaving of British and American humour. Kevin Kline and Jamie Lee Curtis played Otto and Wanda, a pair of American con artists visiting London, who pose as brother and sister. With the help of a stuttering animal lover (Michael Palin) and a cockney thief, Tom Georgeson, they pull off a jewel robbery. In the subsequent confusion the latter, the only one who knows where the loot is stashed, is caught and sent to prison. Wanda tries to find out where it is hidden through his barrister, the stuffy Archie, played by Cleese. He is married to the dreary Wendy, played by Maria Aitken, but Wanda is determined to break down his English reserve and seduce him, with Otto becoming increasingly consumed with violent jealousy.

'Charlie was magnificent. He never shot anything we didn't use, he was editing

LEFT & BELOW Cleese as the hysterically thwarted Stimson in *Clockwise*

If you've ever been late – you'll know what this film is all about...

CLOCKWISE

JOHN CLEESE · JAMIE LEE CURTIS · KEVIN KLINE · MICHAEL PALIN

A tale of murder, greed, lust, revenge and seafood.

A FISH CALLED WANDA

METRO-GOLDWYN-MAYER Presents
A MICHAEL SHAMBERG/PROMINENT FEATURES Production "A FISH CALLED WANDA"
Starring JOHN CLEESE · JAMIE LEE CURTIS · KEVIN KLINE · MICHAEL PALIN
Executive STEVE ABBOTT · JOHN CLEESE Story by JOHN CLEESE & CHARLES CRICHTON
Screenplay by JOHN CLEESE Produced by MICHAEL SHAMBERG Directed by CHARLES CRICHTON
© 1988 METRO-GOLDWYN-MAYER PICTURES, INC. IN ASSOCIATION WITH STAR PARTNERS LIMITED

ABOVE American lobby card for *A Fish Called Wanda*, the most successful British comedy shown there

everything in his head as we went along. Every day we finished at six, and came in under budget.'

A sequel to *A Fish Called Wanda* is in preparation, to be filmed in 1994 with most of the original main cast, the screenplay by Cleese and Iain Johnstone. More films will follow. 'Iain has come up with two wonderful ideas. I really like writing with him. In 1997 we will probably do a farce. I love the energy and intricacy of farce. If you get it right it can be utterly joyous.'

The director of the *Wanda* sequel, which has the working title *Death Fish*, is Robert Young who made the 1993 film *Splitting Heirs*, written by Eric Idle. Cleese appeared in it as a unscrupulous solicitor engaged in assisting Idle to murder his way to an inheritance. It went down well at the Cannes Film Festival where the French found resemblances to *Kind Hearts and Coronets*. More recently Cleese has appeared in *Mary Shelley's Frankenstein*, directed by Kenneth Branagh, and the new Disney live-action version of *The Jungle Book*, directed by Stephen Sommers who had previously directed *The Adventures of Huck Finn*. He also makes frequent appearances in television commercials, including exhorting the public not to smoke, and in the 1992 general election to vote for the Liberal Democrats, and even managed to startle his friends by allowing himself to be photographed for American Express advertising by Annie Leibowitz both in a chic pink drag outfit and in another shot trussed and hanging upside down from a tree.

The death of Graham Chapman in 1989 was a considerable shock to him. Graham had been John's writing partner preceding and during the *Monty Python* years as well as a fellow Footlight in their Cambridge years. During the making of the film *Monty Python and the Holy Grail* his alcoholism became so serious that it nearly killed him then, had he not immediately given up drinking, but it was cancer that eventually ended his life. During his later years John saw little of him, but was understandably distressed, and delivered a memorable, generous and witty address at his memorial service, even to adapting the Parrot Sketch to make his point.

'He and I used to write together from 1962. When the drinking took over and he was scared about his lines he used to drink on the day of the show. At one time we had to abandon a sketch. Things got very awkward when he was drunk. It was extremely difficult having to write with an alcoholic who couldn't remember after lunch what we had written in the morning. And the other Pythons didn't help me out. When he took the decision to dry out he was very brave. He fell over on New Year's Eve in 1977, gashed his head and never drank

again. He was very easy to work with in *The Life of Brian*. I felt much safer with him – he wasn't weird and angry and unpredictable. The sad thing about Graham was that he had a low opinion of himself. He didn't feel very comfortable and I think that is why he drank. He lived in a fantasy world which is why *A Liar's Autobiography* is so great. He could incorporate fantasy without anyone knowing where the line was.

'His death hit me hard, a strong reminder of one's own mortality. I remembered all the good times.'

81

GRAHAM CHAPMAN

BORN 8TH JANUARY 1941
DIED 4TH OCTOBER 1989

LEICESTER
MIDLANDS

The world lost Graham Chapman when cancer claimed him on 4 October 1989, the eve of the twentieth anniversary of *Monty Python's Flying Circus*. Understandably, the celebrations had already been postponed on account of Graham's illness but his death was still a shock for his fellow Pythons. It was not the first time that the Grim Reaper had called for him. In the mid-1970s he had been on the brink of death from chronic alcoholism but with superhuman effort had abruptly stopped drinking, and was so able to rejoin the living, at least for the ensuing twelve years. Sadly, he is the Python who has to be written about in the past tense.

Graham Chapman was tall and craggy, a pipe-smoker who usually gave the impression of calmness; it disguised a dangerously manic unpredictability that was particularly rampant during the drinking years. Interestingly, the circumstances of his birth were far from placid. He arrived on 8 January 1941 during an air raid on the Midlands city of Leicester. He claimed not to have been traumatized by the experience, and the war was a fleeting memory for him. When he was three however, he did recall something unpleasant. 'My father was a policeman, at that stage a constable on the beat in a suburb of Leicester. He had to attend an air crash. There were a lot of pieces of aircraft and people. My father was sent along there to sort it out. I was taken there by my mother who was merely saying hallo to him while he was doing his job. A woman came out of the house carrying a bucket of what looked like liver, and probably was. And there were a number of ominous-looking sacks. That sort of thing would put you off war.'

When his father retired he had reached the rank of chief inspector. 'He wasn't all that authoritarian. He believed in the spirit of the law rather than the letter. He certainly wasn't the kind who chalks up lots of arrests to get promotion. He was pretty easy-going, really. I have to say that there are very few

RIGHT **Graham gave the impression of calmness concealing dangerous unpredicatbility**

LEFT **Annual Shakespeare plays at Melton Mowbray Grammar School exercised his early acting talent**

other policemen I've met I'd like to have had as a father.'

Graham's brother John, four years his senior, had decided to become a doctor. A similar ambition inspired Graham after he started to peruse his brother's medical books. He also took an interest in comedy on the radio and later television. 'Around about the age of fourteen I saw an excerpt on TV of a Footlight show. I think that Jonathan Miller may have been in it. So that slipped into my subconscious, and I thought that if I'm to do medicine then Cambridge is the university.'

Being a policeman, Graham Chapman's father was obliged to move around his county with each posting. Consequently the two boys attended several schools. The most important in Graham's case was Melton Mowbray Grammar School, located in a pleasant market town famous for its meat pies and Britain's largest pet food factory. 'I was comfortable at Melton Mowbray because it was a small town with its own identity. At school I could do a lot of acting – there was a Gilbert and Sullivan each year, and a Shakespeare every year, we also did revues.

RIGHT Graham Chapman in *Cambridge Circus* on Broadway, after touring New Zealand

There were a lot of chances to go over the top. Then a new headmaster, a rather splendid guy called Brewster, encouraged me to go to Cambridge.'

Gaining admission to his chosen ancient university was unexpectedly easy. He went for an interview with the Master of Emmanuel College and was told that he had a place, subject to good A-levels. His rugby-playing was approved, but he was warned off acting, the Master saying that there would be no time for that. 'I'd been briefed that the way to pass the interview was to agree with him most of the time, but to disagree at one point just to show I had a mind of my own. So that's where I differed.'

Within days of his arrival for the Michaelmas Term of 1959 he attended the Societies' Fair at which freshmen were invited to join a broad range of non-academic activities. David Frost, then the club secretary, manned the Footlights stall. 'I asked if I could join. He said "No". So I asked what was the point of having a stall and he said "None at all really," and explained that if one wanted to join one had to be invited to audition. That seemed rather

unattainable, so I joined the Mummers instead. Then I found another guy, called Anthony Branch, at my college who was reading Law and was a bit of a pianist. We teamed up and hit on the idea of holding our own smoking concert to which we invited the Footlights' committee, and we also provided a lot of good claret. They came to our smoker, which was quite a reasonable show, drank our claret, and thus we got our invitation to audition and were duly elected. But by then it was my second year. It was when I met John Cleese – he was auditioning at the same time. Afterwards we compared notes, went off to the Kenya coffee house, and that's how the two of us came to work together. We wrote two or three sketches for smokers that year.'

Although Cleese was still in his freshman year, he had already achieved membership of the Footlights. Eric Idle arrived a year later and was elected following a satisfactory college smoker. Both Cleese and Chapman were on the 1961-2 committee but *Double Take* in 1962 was the only May Week revue in which they both appeared. Also in the cast were Tim Brooke-Taylor, Humphrey Barclay, Tony Hendra, Alan George, Miriam Margolyes, Nigel Brown and Robert Atkins. Trevor Nunn, who directed, re-employed a set consisting of elaborately carved arches that he had previously used for his production of *Much Ado About Nothing*.

Following Cambridge, Graham Chapman continued his medical studies at St Bartholomew's Hospital in London, where his brother had qualified. In 1963 the Footlights show, *A Clump of Plinths* was transferred to the West End, as *Cambridge Circus*. One of its cast, Tony Buffery, dropped out of the show and show business, and Humphrey Barclay invited Graham Chapman to replace him. Bart's operated a tolerant regime, and although hours were long, evenings were the students' own. 'By day I was doing medical clerking and surgical dressing, and by night I was falling around on stage – for about three months. That gave me a big taste for performing, I suppose.'

When the invitation came to tour New Zealand with the show his dilemma was resolved by deciding to take a year off from medicine. By the time that he resumed his studies his alternative existence had become lucrative. He appeared in cabaret at the Blue Angel nightclub, contributed to radio and television comedy shows, including *The Frost Report*, and he was invited to write a series for

BELOW Graham's famous one-man wrestling technique drew the admiration of professional fighters

ABOVE Graham shows How to Hit People Over
the Head while making an arrest under the
Strange Sketch Act in Monty Python

Ronnie Corbett. 'I'd qualified as a doctor and had gone to Ibiza with John, and Marty Feldman was there. David Frost suddenly arrived, and put all these proposals. It was a very exciting period.'

What followed was a film called *The Rise and Rise of Michael Rimmer*, directed by Kevin Billington, a comedy about an efficiency expert who eventually becomes prime minister. It was unsuccessful and its release was so long delayed that the advent of *Monty Python* made its style seem dated.

'I couldn't really see myself doing medicine for the rest of my life. It seemed too ordered, comfortable, protected. I wanted more adventure, some disruption. I had an ear, nose and throat appointment lined up at Bart's which I threw up after I came back from Ibiza. Then I wrote for Roy Hudd, just to see if I could write on my own and not in partnership with John.'

Having qualified as a doctor, he was able to use his medical knowledge for a Humphrey Barclay comedy series at London Weekend based on Richard Gordon's *Doctor* novels. 'John and I were contacted and we did the first episode, using my experience of first days at a hospital. It didn't take more than two or three days to write because it was all there in my head. From thereafter it was a very useful series for John and me. If one was ever short of a bit of loot one could go back and write a few episodes. I did about thirty, I think. It was a nice experience and certainly used up a backlog of medical stories.'

The coming-together of the future Pythons was effected through *The Frost Report*, where Cleese and Chapman began to know the other writing partners, Michael Palin and Terry Jones. I remember thinking "Why does Terry Jones laugh so much?" They couldn't read out their material without laughing all the time. We weren't like that. What was interesting was that out of the twenty or so writers on *The Frost Report* the most prolific ones came together – Michael and Terry used to be very good at writing the bits of film that were used, Eric Idle was excellent at one-liners, and John and I used to go for a more verbal style of comedy – we realized that we all had something different to offer, and Barry Took brought us together with the idea of doing a series. Terry Gilliam I didn't know, but John did, and I think that he was responsible for bringing him into the group.

'We often felt when we were doing *The Frost Report* that some items that we knew were

ABOVE **Graham Chapman interviews Ann Elk (John Cleese) on her Brontosaurus Theory**

87

funny would not get done because it was thought that they were too rude or too silly. And with other people performing what we had written they also injected a lot of themselves into our material and changed it away from what we intended. We thought that apart from enjoying performing we would be able to do it how we wanted – we didn't have to worry about performers because we were going to do it ourselves. We could approach the whole thing as writers. We had much more control.

'I think that it was John who chose Sousa's *Liberty Bell* as our signature tune. He was always fascinated by Sousa.' John Cleese also tended to read the Cleese-Chapman contributions in script conferences in the same way that Terry Jones deferred to Michael Palin. Some of the early *Python* shows used up material that had been originally written for *The Frost Report*. Graham soon noted that it was best to present a piece that required a hard sell before lunch while a silly item went down better after. 'Eric had the most difficult job since he was on his own and didn't have me or Terry Jones to giggle at his stuff'.

The Oxford-Cambridge polarities also became rapidly apparent. 'We regarded the Oxford crowd as more emotional and less logical in their thinking. Cambridge people are more logical and more hidebound in convention and practicalities. The Cambridge people are keen to get out there, do it efficiently, earn some money and look professional. The Oxford ones have more heart, and get more emotionally involved. And they're possibly less self-critical. It's the icy cold winds of the Fens that makes Cambridge different.'

He and John Cleese wrote two or three sketches with biblical themes during their Footlights days and consequently found the construction of *The Life of Brian* relatively easy, with the screenplay taking shape by the time they reached their sunny work station in Barbados. *The Meaning of Life*, on the other hand, was harder because he believed that they were pushed too soon to produce a final draft

BELOW **Graham rests in the filming of The Life of Brian, with Terry Jones, left**

and by the time they were in the Caribbean they had still not achieved a good enough idea. The final film showed signs of hasty assembly. It was also wasteful, with much material excluded because it was seen as irrelevant, not because it was unfunny.

When *The Meaning of Life* was finished Chapman started work on *Yellowbeard*, a pirate comedy which he had written with Peter Cook and Bernard McKenna some years earlier, but had been unable to see into production. In the last week of filming in Mexico Marty Feldman, who had a large part in the film, died following a heartache. 'It was terrible that it should have happened in Mexico City – there was a festival on and it took two

LEFT **Graham Chapman as Brian, mistaken for another who was born in a manger, in** *The Life of Brian*

hours for an ambulance to get through and take him to hospital and it was too late.' He was forty-nine. The tragedy seemed to blight the film which, in spite of the talent involved, turned out fairly disastrously.

Understandably, Graham as a qualified physician would have been concerned over health. Yet ironically he was the one Python who treated his body with the greatest disregard. At Cambridge he had begun to drink heavily, and early in his career his alcoholism became life-threatening. 'It was awful, I was on three pints of gin a day, which is a lot. I came pretty close to snuffing. Because I withdrew myself with no medical attention other than my own, I had three days in bed shivering and hallucinating – objects seemed to move like the way W C Fields shows it when he thinks something is lunging at him when it isn't. Then after three days I stopped shaking and got up. But I hadn't eaten and I was very short of blood sugar. I went into muscular spasm then an epileptic fit. When I came round I realized what a mess alcohol made of the body and that death was very close. That ended it.

'I enjoyed drinking a lot at first. It helped me because I was a quiet reserved person, rather shy. Alcohol does help where social intercourse is concerned. I was affected by my own case, and also the death of a very close friend of mine, Keith Moon. He had had fits too, and had actually bitten clean through his tongue. And yet, even after that he went back to drinking. I know it's a paradox that of all the Pythons I'm the one who knows the body most, and knows what the potential damage is, but oddly enough, I felt I could handle it – I take all the vitamin pills and watch for the danger signs.'

'I remember on the first day of filming *Holy Grail*, seven o'clock in the morning on a Scottish hillside, and nothing to drink – I suddenly had DTs. I was playing King Arthur in a cold drizzle, and I realized I was letting my friends down, and letting myself down. I stayed more or less on an even keel, not drinking too much, but I resolved to stop as soon as I could.' His semi-autobiography, *A Liar's Auto-biography* while for the most part wildly improbable, is not completely without any semblance of truth. John Cleese felt that it was an appropriate narrative. 'The

sad thing is that Graham had a low opinion of himself and that is why he drank. He lived in a fantasy world, which is why *A Liar's Autobiography* is great. He could incorporate fantasy without anyone knowing what the line was.'

Graham at least was frank about his alcoholism, and used his experiences to help others. He was equally honest where his homosexuality was concerned, but denied that it had any connection with his drinking. 'I was an early campaigner for gay liberation. I realized some of the problems people had – I hadn't suffered them particularly, and the line of work I had opted for was probably the most tolerant towards that kind of behaviour – certainly medicine wasn't, which made me angry, because these were the people who should have been compassionate and understanding, and they were just being fascist as far as I could see. So that led to a kind of anger, which expressed itself in terms of buying tea urns for the Gay Liberation Front, and going to meetings, and wearing over-flowery trousers and generally being obnoxious to people in pubs. At one time my friends needed to protect me, I was such a danger. I remember being in a pub in Chalk Farm, and there had just been an England-Scotland football match. I was wearing the statutory flowery shirt and playing bar billiards when I heard a Glaswegian gentleman talking to his mate, say something about "Jessie". So I went over to him and said

"Why sneer at Jessies? I'm one," not quite knowing if I was going to get a bottle in my face. "Look, I'm a Jessie, I'm a homosexual." There was a pause while he looked at me, then he said "Och, that was fockin' brave. Let me buy ye a drink."'

He was twenty-five when he had first decided to give homosexuality a try, having up to that point regarded himself as an uncertain hetero. 'I was amazed at the similarity. The emotional relationships are slightly more intense, maybe because it's frowned upon by the rest of society. It didn't seem unnatural. It's something that very many people know about but pretend not to – they've indulged in it at school to an extent, not enough to make them homosexuals, but it does mean they know about it. The most important thing is that it's about being with someone with whom you click, someone you find physically and mentally attractive and you have a good time.'

For two decades he lived with David Sherlock, a relationship he claimed settled into that of any married couple, with each partner moving in slightly different directions. 'There are no rules for me, and I don't try to find any. But it does make me a bit of an outsider. And possibly I can observe others from a different standpoint which is useful. I don't necessarily accept what other people say as being the way things are in their relationships. What fascinated me in the beginning was not so much the difference, but the similarity. I'm not at all interested in procreation – I don't feel the need to reproduce myself around the earth, I don't know how I would feel if there was another little Chapman wandering around.

'There was no problem with the other Pythons when I told them. John was the only one who was very, very surprised and shocked. Marty just laughed. But they could have been amazed – here was a pipe-smoking rugby player, keen on mountaineering. Jonathan Miller said I was a little unfair, presenting such a front to the world and then doing a turnaround. But I felt that the climate was right to come out, it was a cause I could do something for. I met Mrs Mary Whitehouse of the National Viewers and Listeners Association once, and was surprised as most people are, and reasonably charmed by the

LEFT Carolyn Seymour, Snoopy and Graham Chapman in *The Odd Job*

91

lady. We talked about plants in Australia, nothing germane to the real nitty-gritty.'

Graham's assessment of the lady was premature, as it happened. In 1972 he had co-founded *Gay News* and had given the publication considerable financial support. Later Mrs Whitehouse arranged a private prosecution when it published a poem which she considered blasphemous. Although Graham did not like the poem very much, he deplored her attempt to stifle free speech.

He remembered taking part in an informal television programme hosted by George Melly in which the talk came around to the topic of being gay. A woman viewer wrote in complaining that someone from the *Monty Python* team who had not had the courage to give his name – which was of course untrue – had confessed to his homosexuality, and she enclosed a bundle of payers for the salvation of his soul, as well as a biblical quotation: 'If a man lie with another he shall be taken out and killed.' The letter was forwarded to the *Python* office where it fell to Eric Idle's lot to compose a reply. It was to the effect: 'We have found out who it is and we've taken him out and killed him.'

There were Pythons at his bedside as he died. His throat cancer had become acute in the late summer of 1989 and he underwent painful and distressing treatment. A few weeks before the end he was interviewed for NBC's *Entertainment Tonight*, looking gaunt and weak, but optimistically claiming to be licking it. In the days before he died he observed that he had just had the most interesting year of his life. David Sherlock and Graham's adopted son, John Tomiczek, together with the Pythons, organized an unorthodox memorial service at Bart's at which they delivered their favourite Graham Chapman anecdotes. Others present included Barry Cryer, Tim Brooke-Taylor, Douglas Adams, Carol Cleveland and a large number of friends and associates. Neil Innes, wearing a duck hat, sang 'It's Sweet to be an Idiot' and Eric Idle wound up the proceedings by leading all of those present in a hearty rendering of 'Always Look on the Bright Side of Life'. That evening the Pythons staged their postponed twentieth anniversary party at Porchester Hall, Bayswater. Graham would certainly have enjoyed it.

OPPOSITE **Graham as *Yellowbeard* the pirate**

TOP **The British poster** BELOW **Graham and Beryl Reid in *Yellowbeard***

ERIC IDLE

Two writing partnerships were absorbed into the Pythons – John Cleese and Graham Chapman, Terry Jones and Michael Palin. That left Terry Gilliam in his own corner, a sensible position in view of the arcane nature of his contribution, which in any case was graphic rather than verbal – and Eric Idle. Eric was content to be cast as the group loner, preferring to write by himself at his own pace, although he sometimes found it difficult in having to present his material to the others and make it seem funny without the back-up support of a partner. 'It was easier with a show where there were thirteen in a series than with a film, where stuff was read out all the time, and you had to convince five others. And they were not the most unegotistical of writers, either.'

His participation was essential to the Python synergy. His talent for verbal humour is exceptional. As a performer he has the ability to master with ease tongue-twisting wordplays that verge on impossibility. He is a songwriter with an ear for lyrics, and the facility to parody popular styles with a degree of affection for their kind. Among his many skills he is also an accomplished guitarist.

BORN 29TH MARCH 1943

SOUTH SHIELDS
COUNTY DURHAM

Eric Idle was the last Python to leave his university, having gone up to Cambridge when John Cleese was in his final year and Graham Chapman had already gone down. In 1964-5 he took over the presidency of the Footlights from Graeme Garden who had in turn succeeded Tim Brooke-Taylor, and his fellow cast members in the 1965 May Week revue, *My Girl Herbert*, included Clive James, Germaine Greer, John Cameron and John Grillo. The main mark of his presidency was to secure full membership for women.

He was born in South Shields, County Durham on 29 March 1943. When he was two his father, who had been serving in the Royal Air Force, was killed in a car crash. 'It was Christmas

RIGHT **Eric Idle, *Python* loner, songwriter, parodist, tongue-twisting wordsmith**

94

ABOVE Eric Idle in *My Girl Herbert*, Cambridge
Footlights 1965, Clive James behind him,
John Cameron at piano

Eve, which meant a bleak Christmas for my mother, at least.' He was educated at the Royal School, Wolverhampton, described by him as a Midlands semi-orphanage. Among its earlier pupils was the poet and novelist Philip Oakes who, in an autobiographical account, described it in horrific terms. The harsh regime was easier in Eric Idle's time, he claims because they had run out of orphans, although the fabric of the buildings remained oppressive. He remembers the Victorian dormitories a hundred yards long. It was his home for twelve years from the age of seven onwards. His quick intelligence enabled him to maintain a steady academic progress, in spite of illicit nocturnal swimming parties with girls from their adjoining school, and he decided to try for Cambridge.

'I had to meet three people for the interview at Pembroke College. One was an Arabic scholar, one was a professor of Economics, and one was a mathematician. And I was going to read English, right? So we discussed what was on in the West End, which I happened to know – it was all we could talk about. Pembroke is a comedians' college. Peter Cook was there. I got through on the interview, I could never have passed the exams. It was odd but to be encouraged, I think, that kind of selection.

'I'd never heard of the Footlights when I got there, but we had a tradition of college smoking-concerts, and I sent in some sketches parodying a play that had just been done. Tim Brooke-Taylor and Bill Oddie auditioned me for the Footlights smoker, and that led to me discovering about and getting into the Footlights, which was great. One could go and lunch in their clubroom, and swan in at about eleven at night and stay drinking until three. Lion's Yard was terrific, alas all gone.'

His time in the Footlights trailed in the shadow of John Cleese, and at his first Pembroke smoker Eric performed an old sketch by his predecessor, in which an Old Testament prophet delivers the weather forecast. Cleese was not allowed to perform at Pembroke because it was not his college. 'In fact John spent more time at Pembroke than Downing. He used to dine at Pembroke nearly every night, and some of the dons actually thought that he was a Pembroke man. John was a very conservative figure in those days, wore tweed suits and belonged to the Pitt Club. He's always had that streak, half caught by it, half despising it. He's the

BELOW **A stoney-faced Idle in *We Have Ways of Making You Laugh*, 1968**

closest thing to the English class system. He ought to be Sir John or Baron Cleese of Notting Hill.'

The other conditioning factor during Eric's Footlights presidency was the eruption of the new spirit of liberation that characterized 1960s Britain. With hemlines rising towards the navel, pirate radio wavelengths dominated by Liverpudlian pop groups, the incoming Prime Minister Harold Wilson endlessly espousing the new classlessness and visualizing a Britain swept forward by the white heat of technology, admitting women to the Footlights was an irresistible nod to the mood of the times.

'Several of the gay dons were in tears when women came in, and they'd say things like "Binky will simply die" ['Binky' Beaumont was a leading West End impresario around whom a homosexual coterie hung]. Me, in my little leather jacket, I was totally unsympathetic. Germaine Greer came into the club at the same time as Clive James. She was a very funny

ABOVE **Eric Idle in bed with Carol Cleveland and Terry Jones for a** *Python* **sketch**

97

ABOVE **Eric Idle as a marriage guidance counsellor takes a fancy to the wife, Carol Cleveland**

lady. After doing a striptease out of a nun's habit she'd be down to a bikini and would put flippers on to go swimming. We toured England to various exotic locations such as Worcester and Ipswich, and we just limped in near the West End for three patchy weeks at the Lyric, Hammersmith with *A Girl Called Herbert*, a show only worth vaguely remembering.

'Then John Cameron and I went to The Blue Angel where we auditioned on a Saturday – it was a way they got a free cabaret when the place was packed. We took the place apart, we were wonderful. So we were booked for two weeks from the Monday. On the Monday night the audience was three Guards officers, two debs and eight bottles of champagne, and it's

98

death for the rest of the week, not a titter. Then Richard Eyre did *Oh! What a Lovely War* at Leicester and called in all sorts of Cambridge people for it – it was an amazing production where every night the cast cried more than the audience, we were all so terrifically motivated, while they left for early buses. Then I got conned to stay for *One for the Pot*, which was possibly one of the worst parts ever written – I played a character who became notorious for not being on stage, and I would get so bored and be sitting in the dressing-room writing sketches, until one night an actor I was supposed to be on with came all the way up and said "Would you mind joining me on stage?" I realized I didn't want to put up with being an actor. I was writing sketches for *I'm Sorry, I'll Read That Again* which they bought, then for Frosty and *The Frost Report*.'

Working on Frost's Continuously Developing Monologue with its escalatory absurdism was an excellent exercise for Eric Idle's comic skills, and brought him in contact with the other future Pythons. This was followed by Humphrey Barclay's Rediffusion show, *Do Not Adjust Your Set,* his first encounter with Neil Innes, then with the Bonzo Dog Band, with whom he would collaborate on his mock-Beatles documentary, *The Rutles.* Also in the team were Michael Palin and Terry Jones, alongside David Jason and Denise Coffey as the non-Oxbridge performers. Ironically the show was originally regarded as being for children, and was scheduled early in the evening's viewing time, although it soon attained a following among

BELOW **A toupeed Idle is confronted by shoddily-toupeed toupee salesmen**

adults who would rush home from work for it. The second series was produced by Thames who inherited Rediffusion's London television channel. Then came another Barclay show hosted by Frank Muir, *We Have Ways of Making You Laugh*, which was a mixture of improvised talk and prepared sketches. Terry Gilliam had become the show's instant cartoonist, and was delighted that Eric was unfazed by his bizarre appearance and Californian accent. At Eric's urging Gilliam was included in Barry Took's line-up for the show that became *Monty Python's Flying Circus*.

Gilliam's inclusion had another happy outcome. Cleese and Chapman were a team, Palin and Jones were a team, Idle was a loner as was Gilliam, and each represented an opposite strand of humour. Idle's was intellectually based, logically formed and razor-sharp. Gilliam's was anarchic, zany,

ABOVE **A rest on the
Jabberwocky set**

earthy and even mildly scatological. In a curious way it made them compatible within the group's structure.

At the end of the third series when John Cleese upset the symmetry by leaving, Eric was tempted to follow. He bided his time until the fourth series had ended, then persuaded BBC2 to run a weekly half-hour series called *Rutland Weekend Television*, a parody of a commercial station based in Britain's smallest county. The budget was minute, which in a way fitted the impoverished ethos of the station, and Eric Idle played most of the parts, with Neil Innes supplying musical items, including pastiches of popular songs. In 1976 Eric was invited to host an edition of the NBC comedy show *Saturday Night Live* in New York and included in it a joke film with Neil Innes which sent up the Beatles and *A Hard Day's Night*. The executive producer, Lorne Michaels, was so impressed that he commissioned a full-length bogus documentary for Eric to direct on an NBC budget. It was *The Rutles: All You Need is Cash*, which featured *Saturday Night Live* regulars such as Dan Aykroyd, Gilda Radner and John Belushi and appearances by Mick Jagger, Paul Simon and George Harrison. Following the Beatles story closely, it exposed the media circus (Rutlemania) and the financial mismanagement that precipitated the group's demise, with mock archive footage and devastatingly accurate parodies of their films, with the titles *A Hard Day's Rut, Ouch!, Tragical History Tour* (their first flop), *Yellow Submarine Sandwich* and *Let it Rut*. Record albums and a video inevitably followed. Much of the cleverness of *The Rutles* derived from the close adherence to the style of Beatles' graphics, posters, record sleeves and so on.

Innes was given his own BBC series, *The Innes Book of Records*, after its success, and Eric Idle was later to use his friendship with the ex-Beatle George Harrison to extricate the Pythons from difficulties when EMI pulled out of *The Life of Brian*. HandMade Films started as a consequence.

For Eric films were a logical progression. At the time of *The Meaning of Life* he said: 'When I look at the *Fringe* group, Peter Cook and the others, and see they're not together, I can see the value in having to lose your ego like us, and come together and suffer a little and produce work – it's actually reassuring as you get older. The older John gets, the more it will be

pleasant for him to realize that he isn't just a loony – there are five other loonies with him, and we can't all be completely mad if we agree. Comedy is something where you suffer for other people – there's something involved in being up to your neck in muck which makes people laugh. John is wonderful, he's enormously talented and funny, has a tremendously bleak view of life, and he isn't going to be remembered by posterity for his Sony commercials. He needs to have his rear end kicked sometimes to produce this kind of work, even if it means roughing it.

We are all super-critical about each other – the day we say "Wonderful, darling!" and become like Richard Attenborough we're sunk. I think it's the important thing – we do all keep a strong critical eye on what everyone else is doing. It's healthy, and if you're reading a script out to everyone and something doesn't work, it's better to get that sort of criticism while you're still making the film than when it is out – at least you have the chance to make it better.'

BELOW **Accountancy shanties, as presented by Rutland Weekend Television**

Sometimes interviewers have been surprised by the Pythons' candour about each other, uncommon in a business where gushing bonhomie in public conceals ugly realities. The Pythons often disagree but retain an essential respect for each other. The commonest moan about Eric is that he was the one who remained most aloof from the nuts-and-bolts mundanity of film-making. While Terry Jones was frantically trying to achieve a final cut on *The Meaning of Life* Eric was wintering in Australia. 'Terry constantly changes his mind on tiny details. To be around watching minor changes is a totally frustrating experience,' commented Eric. 'Towards the end he is much more in need of support and a fresh eye, hence I thought to stay away and come home in March. The advancing of the deadline meant that instead of coming in at the right time I could see the rough cut only on video in Sydney. I still feel that what I saw there was better than the final cut.'

He has vivid memories of the time when Graham Chapman made public his homosexuality. 'I didn't know, even when I

was writing with him. He was leading an incredible double life. He had this wonderful party where he decided to tell everybody. It was a very interesting evening. For a long time, I think because of the alcohol, we never got on, we were close to fighting a lot of the time. When he became sober that ceased to happen. Anyway, I remember at that party he suddenly said "I want you all to meet the man I love." I knew at once that it wasn't a joke, that he was deadly serious. Marty Feldman was very good about it, but there was a girl there who was in love with Graham and she was weeping, absolutely distraught. Marty, who was then our script editor, said that we weren't to start making poof jokes, that it shouldn't make any difference. He was right, of course. If you're working with someone their sex life isn't what counts, it's the quality of their ideas, what they can offer. But writing teams are like marriages, they go through their moods and break up – Marty and Barry Took, Michael and Terry, Graham and John.'

While unenthusiastic about scriptwriting partnerships Eric has had two marriages, the first to an Australian actress, Lyn Ashley in 1969. Their son Carey was born in

BELOW **Rutland Weekend Television beauty contest with Eric Idle as hayseed presenter**

1973, but two years later they were divorced. He met his present wife, Tania, during his *Saturday Night Live* days in New York in 1977, and they have a daughter, Lily, born in 1990. He has a theory, which would appear to be supported by John Cleese, that Englishmen should never marry Englishwomen because they make the wrong kind of noises together. 'Tania's a perfect American. Her mother's Italian and her father's Russian. She's not in show business, she is not impressed by it. She's rarely interested in what I write – eventually I'll force her to read something. She's perfectly normal, balanced and sane. She's lovely, what more can I say?'

Another of his theories is that the nicest, most interesting British people don't live in their homeland. He divides his time between London and California, where he has a house in the San Fernando Valley, which was affected by the 1994 earthquake. 'I really appreciate England when I'm travelling around the world. The best Englishmen are the expatriates – they're wonderful people. This is a small island. The options after you have done a series of your own are not that open. I think it's more challenging to keep moving. I like working with people who are good – I think that the Pythons are much the best in the country, probably the best, and I like to meet people who are that serious about their business in other parts of the world.'

He has made a number of films in the post-*Python* years, including the successful *Nuns on the Run* with Robbie Coltrane, written and directed by Jonathan Lynn. They played a pair of small-time hoods who for reasons of plot flee their murderous pursuers by hiding in a convent, where they don habits to pass themselves off as visiting sisters from another order. This was followed by the less successful *Splitting Heirs*, which he executive produced and wrote. As a producer he was responsible for an innovative British comedy of 1992, *Leon the Pig Farmer*. In another direction, he scored a considerable success as Ko-Ko in Jonathan Miller's glittering 1920s production of Gilbert and Sullivan's *The Mikado* for the English National Opera, a reminder of his musical skills (he is the only Python to have had a song-hit in the charts, 'Always Look on the Bright Side of Life'.) He also had a play performed in the West End in 1981, *Pass the Butler,* and has published several books, mostly *Python* compilations, and a novel, *Hello Sailor.*

'Writing is such a sedentary, debilitating experience. In England I try very hard. I wrote a play because I thought that

LEFT **Eric Idle as Ko-Ko in The Mikado**

103

the West End was dying on its feet – all those empty theatres and actors unemployed. I wrote a play which was a very interesting and enjoyable experience, until it came into the West End when we were shat upon from a great height. If I did a play now I wouldn't even bring it into the West End. I would just tour England with it. Coming in is so prohibitive, so expensive, that you are much better off taking plays round where people can see them more easily. I'll always love the theatre for giving me my first break. *Beyond the Fringe* was a big moment for me. Everyone talks about the Goons – but the Goons didn't mean that much to me. However, when I saw *Beyond the Fringe*, that was it, it was so very, very funny about taboo subjects.

'The Goons came from radio and tried to adapt their stuff to television, and that was difficult. We Pythons didn't have that obsession – we were writing for television and could see the potential for what you could do with it. We were the first people, really, after *TW3* to play with the toys. And when we had exhausted what we could do with television we stared to explore film.'

LEFT **Jonathan Miller's production of *The Mikado* provided a rare opportunity for Idle to exercise his musical skills**

LEFT **With Robbie
Coltrane in** *Nuns on
the Run*, **Jonathan
Lynn's comic hit, 1990**

105

PYTHON

It could so easily have been *Owl-Stretching Time*, which is what the Cambridge element wanted to call it. Or *The Year of the Stoat*. Or *The Venus de Milo Panic Show*. John Cleese rather liked the idea of a football team's forward line *Bunn, Wackett, Buzzard, Stubble and Boot*. Michael Mills, the head of comedy at the BBC, described Barry Took as someone who when making a request was really giving an order, just like Baron von Richthofen. Or Baron von Took. It was the germ that produced *Baron von Took's Flying Circus* and was even designated as such on memos, eventually becoming abbreviated to *Flying Circus*. Some theorists believed that *Cambridge Circus* had an influence. Michael Palin was entranced by the name Gwen Dibley, which he had spotted in a local newspaper. For a while the show looked as though it might be called *Gwen Dibley's Flying Circus*. During discussions the name Monty was bandied around, and it was considered suggestive of a shady theatrical booker, who might be fixing a fourth-rate act for a working men's club in Worthington. From there it was but a single step to the magical word Python, itself an unlikely surname, but when combined with Monty, an unusually resonant and pleasing name. Accordingly the show was given its title. Into the dustbin went a proposal that it would be called something different each week, a notion that had caused consternation in the scheduling department at the BBC.

At Eric Idle's instigation Terry Gilliam was introduced into the group to provide its graphics, starting with the credit titles, which were to be constructed with animated collages. The writhing tendrils, dancing heads and gaudy lettering were counterpointed by the strains of Sousa's jaunty march *Liberty Bell* which proved to be an inspired choice as a signature tune. Since the advent of *Monty Python* it has been virtually impossible for the band of the Grenadier Guards to include it in their

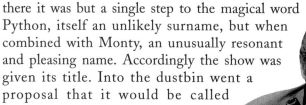

BELOW Terry Gilliam's animated graphics were a successful fusion of sound, crude cutout techniques, and inspiration

ABOVE The famous Python foot, to be found in Bronzino's painting of Venus and Cupid in the National Gallery, London

repertoire without creating an inappropriate stir among onlookers. Michael Palin remembers it being heard in the background of the interview given to the television by the Prince of Wales and his bride Diana at the time of their wedding, as a guards band rehearsed below their window in the evening sunshine. The *Python* title sequence ended with a large foot descending from above, to a raspberry sound effect.

Gilliam, initially not credited with the others but given a subsidiary billing, was accorded the job of creating animation links, which could be surrealistic and absurd, with the purpose of propelling the thrust of the show into unpredictable directions. It was a style to affect the character of the entire show, which was free-form and not confined within a regular format.

ABOVE **Gilliam's linking sequences brought another element of lunacy to the *Python* programmes**

Terry Jones remembered watching *Q5*, Spike Milligan's show. 'He'd got it all – scenery being pushed off the set in mid-sentence, sketches abandoned in the middle and completely new ones taking over. Spike was doing what we wanted to do. We'd all been writing cliches – sketches with beginnings, middles and ends – and suddenly there was Milligan doing this amazing stuff. I remembered an elephant animation Terry Gilliam had done for *Do Not Adjust Your Set* – it was a sort of stream-of-consciousness of disconnected images, using Terry's stuff to link them all together. Milligan had shown us how you could end sketches in the middle without it really mattering – so I talked to Mike Palin about it. The three of us felt that this was the shape, the right thing. But it was a bit of a fight when we started into the shows. John tolerated the idea, but felt that it was the sketches that mattered.'

The producer and director of the first four programmes was John Howard Davies, who in 1948 had played Oliver Twist in David Lean's film of the same name. Ian McNaughton took over from him with the fifth programme. He had been the director of Milligan's *Q5*, and was rapidly able to fall into the *Python* style.

Its debut on BBC television, the first transmission of *Monty Python's Flying Circus*, occurred on 5 October 1969, which was a Sunday, in a slot that up until then had been taken by the repeat of a religious discussion earlier in the evening. The decision to replace it in favour of entertainment had, astonishingly, upset a few diehards who still held to the Reithian idea

that Sundays were for enlightenment and uplift, not pleasure. The Pythons introduced themselves with a new catchphrase designed to mock the tones of a BBC announcer: 'And now for something completely different'. These words would usually be uttered by John Cleese in a dinner jacket as a continuity announcer in an unlikely setting such as the middle of a field, a seashore or a lake. The shows were not aired in the order in which they were recorded but shuffled to maximize the largest audience. The programme recorded second actually went on first and included such *Python* favourites as: 'It's the Arts', a take-off of a TV programme in which John Cleese was an interviewer anxious to know how he was to address his distinguished guest, instead of getting on with things, and the funniest joke in the world, a gag of such potency that the listener would fall about with laughter, and die. When translated into German, it could be used as a secret weapon against the Nazis, who apparently were working on their own joke when they were defeated in 1945. (For the curious the joke was: 'Wenn ist das Nunstück git und Slotermeyer? Ja! ... Beiherhund das Oder die Flipperwaldt gersput.' To be used with caution.) In the second transmitted programme were Arthur Ewing and his Musical Mice, a character played by Terry Jones who renders 'The Bells of St Mary's' by bashing each of the unfortunate (but happily, unseen) animals with a mallet; the marriage guidance counsellor sketch with Michael Palin and Carol Cleveland (who would become the stock Python female for scenes that they could not play convincingly themselves in drag) visiting Eric Idle for advice, only for him to make a bold and reciprocated pass at her; a man with three buttocks; and a parody of *The World Around Us* about men and mice, famous men who have been mice, men who dress as mice and squeak and eat cheese.

Although parodies of television programmes were a staple of *Python* humour, it was not a particularly original comic form. What the Pythons did, however, was to provide opportunities to reach uncharted depths of absurdity within a recognizable and respected format. Sometimes madmen and freaks would be paraded before sombre anchormen, at others it was the interviewer who was clearly insane. The very essence of television could be mocked. A quiz show for instance had Mao, Lenin, Karl Marx and Che Guevara eagerly vying to answer complex questions on English league football, and deftly caught the inane tone of such programmes.

LEFT Terry Gilliam's graphics regularly appeared on the cover of magazines

BELOW The June 1979 edition of the Radio Times announcing a 'rare reunion' of the Pythons

109

Says Barry Took: 'Much of *Python* comedy is simple reversal. Take Hell's Grannies. That's straight out of the Child's Book of How to Write Comedy. Thugs beating up old ladies? Why not have old ladies ganging up, roaming the streets looking for thugs to bash, young people to bully? But it's the way they do it that's so good.'

Another *Python* sketch format used in many variations is that in which an interviewer sits in an office and deals with a visitor. A vocational guidance counsellor conducts a discussion with an accountant who wants to be a lion-tamer. A distinguished explorer who has double vision requests a candidate, whom he insists on addressing in the plural, to climb a twin-peaked mountain. The classic of this particular genre is the sketch in which the man at the desk conducts an argument for a fee.

At the beginning Michael Palin and Terry Jones lobbied for plenty of filmed sequences and these were directed by Ian McNaughton before he became responsible for overseeing the entire show. It was customary for comedy programmes produced by the BBC to use nearby locations in the streets of Acton, Ealing and Shepherds Bush because they were within easy distance of the studios, and on rare occasions go no further afield than the nearby Home Counties. *Python* broke away altogether from this tradition and often took the cameras into the wilds of Britain that were hitherto unknown to the personnel involved, who then found themselves subjected to extreme discomfort on uninhabited Yorkshire moors and rain-sodden Scottish Highland glens. The results were worth the suffering, and *Python* locations always looked interesting.

For the first series a strange, hairy creature was evolved by Michael Palin and called the Hermit. Smeared with dirt, his matted, unkempt hair falling about his face and shoulders, he would haul himself into view in some rugged and remote landscape and make his way towards the camera, encountering a number of dangerous and strange hazards, and gasp 'Its ... !' before collapsing. At this point Terry Gilliam's opening title animation would erupt and another voice, usually that of John Cleese, would announce 'Monty Python's Flying Circus!' And then the *Liberty Bell* march would strike up.

The Pythons were cavalier in their treatment of titles. Sometimes the programme's end credits would appear in the middle of the show, or even at the beginning. They could be in the form of anagrams (there was an extraordinary Eric Idle interview in

BELOW A script conference for the fourth series. Director, Ian MacNaughton, Jones, Chapman, Palin and Neil Innes

which he appeared as a man who spoke only in anagrams, and was working on an anagram version of *Hamlet*: 'Thamle...be ot or bot neot, tath is the nestquie.') or in mock German, pseudo-Scandinavian and even sign language. There was a tendency, even as the last credit had rolled up and the BBC copyright line had appeared, to insert a hanging gag, causing headaches for the continuity staff waiting to announce the succeeding programme. The BBC1 logo of that period, which was a rotating globe against an attenuated and distorted reflection of itself, was frequently used to its disadvantage, and the conventions of the BBC Nine O'Clock News presentation were also constantly sent up. Ten years after *Python* an entire comedy series by a

ABOVE **Customer, Eric Idle, irritates shopkeeper, John Cleese, by only talking in verse**

111

subsequent team was called *Not the Nine O'Clock News*, but they were happy to acknowledge that the Pythons were there first.

The stock figures began to take shape. Among them was a band of strident, domineering, middle-aged women known to the group as Pepperpots, presumably a reference to their shape. It was a group of such ladies (the Pythons relishing their opportunities to indulge in female impersonation) who as the Batley townswomen's guild would restage the battle of Pearl Harbor in mud. There was a masculine counterpart, the Gumbies, a group of lower-middle class men who wore gumboots, rolled their trousers tightly above their knees, sported Fair Isle pullovers over white shirts with rolled up sleeves, and on their heads wore white handkerchiefs, each corner tied in a knot. The prototypical Gumby is alleged to have been spotted by someone on the beach of Margate, but it is much more likely to have been an atavistic memory of Michael Palin, imagining some pre-war filing clerk at the seaside.

Graham Chapman, having created the persona of the pipe-smoking reasonable man, also devised a bristling, indignant colonel in uniform complete with red tabs, who would sometimes march on in the middle of sketches and demand that they be instantly halted on the grounds that they were silly. Another way the Pythons cleverly avoided the need for punch lines was to conclude proceedings abruptly by dropping a sixteen-ton weight onto the cast. Each Python developed a characteristic mode. John Cleese became famous, possibly notorious, for his idiotic department of the civil service, the Ministry of Silly Walks. Its staff were obliged to move grotesquely, their legs splayed in all directions, and Cleese's spider-like gangliness was admirably suited. Terry Jones, stocky, dark, voluble and extremely Welsh, was particularly renowned for his portrayal of shrill, shrieking women. Possibly his most bizarre characterization was that of the naked, smirking organist, first seen in the audience participation show, *Blackmail*.

The first series contained what would become the best-known of all *Python* sketches, the one that involved a pet shop proprietor played by Michael Palin, having an exchange with an indignant customer, John Cleese, who complains that he has been sold a dead parrot, an

ABOVE **A particularly greasy looking Palin**

MONTY PYTHON

ABOVE **John Cleese introduces And Now For Something Completely Different**

113

RIGHT **Michael Palin and wife make a visit to the marriage guidance counsellor who...**

LEFT **... performs quite a different kind of counselling**

114

BELOW **The collision of polite society and bloody gore was a favourite Python preoccupation**

ABOVE **Three Pythons in one body:** *Monty Python and the Holy Grail*

LEFT Without arms or legs, the Knight still wants to fight

FAR LEFT The filming of the *Holy Grail* was arduous with itchy costumes and hostile locations

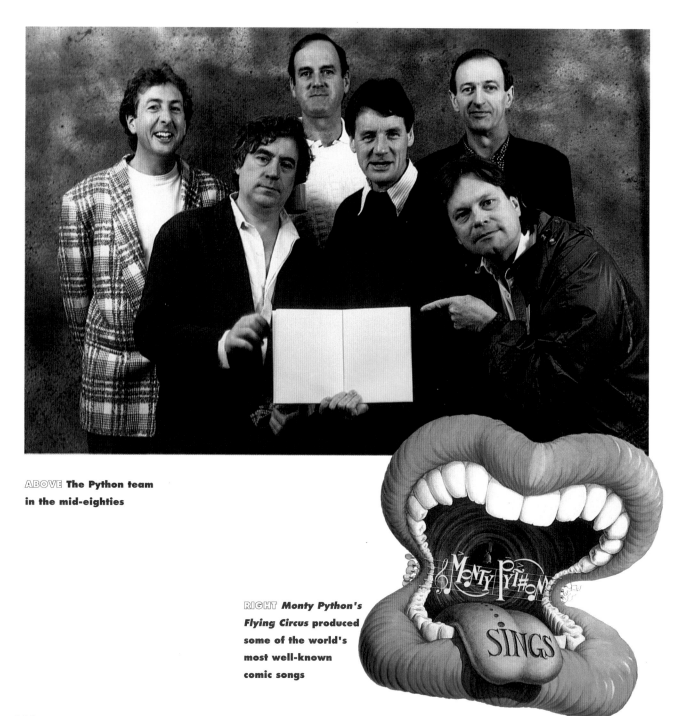

ABOVE **The Python team in the mid-eighties**

RIGHT ***Monty Python's Flying Circus* produced some of the world's most well-known comic songs**

MONTY PYTHON

LEFT Eric Idle, George
Harrison and John Cleese
take a break in the
filming of *The Life of
Brian*

BOTTOM The
controversial finale
to *The Life of Brian*

RIGHT **Graham Chapman performs an impromtu operation in** *The Meaning of Life*

121

MONTY PYTHON

LEFT AND FAR LEFT
The Meaning of Life
was written as a
series of sketches
which included a Las
Vegas style view of
heaven

BELOW Tiger and Palin
in *The Meaning of Life*

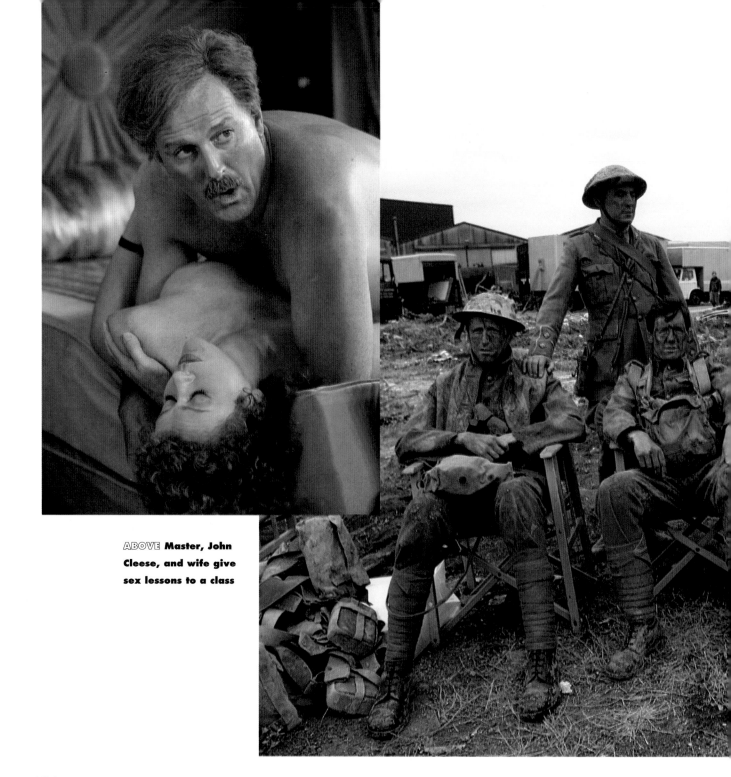

ABOVE **Master, John Cleese, and wife give sex lessons to a class**

124

LEFT First World War costumes and a modern day background, on location for *The Meaning of Life*

BELOW The old insurance firm prepares to set sail in Gilliam's opening short for *The Meaning of Life*

JOHN CLEESE

125

RIGHT One of the more indescribable moments from *The Meaning of Life*

LEFT John Cleese unwisely offers Mr Creosote a wafer-thin mint ...

assertion that is discounted with increasing desperation. Cleese's accelerating protest culminates with the lines:

> 'It's not pining, It's passed on. This parrot is no more. It has ceased to be. It's expired and gone to meet its maker. This is a late parrot. It's a stiff. Bereft of life, it rests in peace. If you hadn't nailed it to its perch, it would be pushing up the daisies. It's rung down the curtain and joined the choir invisible. This is an ex-parrot.'

The simplicity of the two-handed sketch was deceptive. At the time there was no indication that it would become so celebrated, even to at one point being invoked by prime minister Margaret Thatcher during one of her political speeches, since it looked very like many other *Python* sketches.

LEFT ... with the consequent explosive result

The climate at the BBC during this period was much in the Pythons' favour. Interference was initially minimal, and they were allowed to get on with the series more or less as they wanted. The influence of Hugh Greene, the liberal-minded director-general who had left in April 1969, still prevailed for a while, partly because Huw Wheldon, then the managing director of television, went to some trouble to see that judgements were supported, not sabotaged. The Pythons' main grumble was not over artistic inter-ference, but on the constantly shifting transmission time. Not only was it inconsistent each week, but

BELOW Chapman engrossed in the contents of a tabloid newspaper

sometimes it would slip from the schedules altogether for a two-week gap to accommodate some sporting event, or other occasion deemed more important, making it much harder to establish its regular audience. In the circumstances they did reasonably well, lifting their ratings from one to three million, and thereby easily justifying a second series. They were also rewarded with a higher budget and a fixed weekly transmission slot. The latter proved to be a dubious advantage when it was found that the hour chosen, after 10 pm, was the time of regional switching, in which the network fragmented into local programmes. Consequently, the first time round only London and the North saw *Monty Python* and the rest of Britain had to wait for the repeats.

It was an immediate hit with most television critics. Stanley Reynolds in *The Times* for instance, wrote: 'It would still be an incredible bargain for the BBC at twice the price.' Inevitably, there were some dissenters, including Milton Shulman in the London *Evening Standard* who commented: 'The chief fault of *Monty Python's Flying Circus* is that it occasionally reveals an inability to recognize a good joke from a bad one and will stretch unpromising ideas to almost unbearable limits.' In the *Daily Mail* Virginia Ironside was perturbed by the tendency to abort sketches for 'being silly' before they had time to reach a punchline, saying, 'I have always sat through the show with a distinct sneer playing round my mouth.'

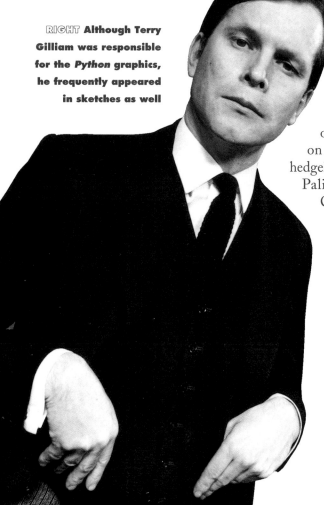

RIGHT **Although Terry Gilliam was responsible for the *Python* graphics, he frequently appeared in sketches as well**

The Pythons' devotees usually regard the second series as the highwater mark, and it is a view that the members themselves echo. The level of invention is extremely high, as is the self-assurance. Again, the shows were not transmitted in the order in which they were recorded. Silly Walks appeared in the first on the air, as did Spiny Norman, Terry Gilliam's fearsome giant hedgehog. The Spanish Inquisition, a trio of scarlet-robed cardinals – Palin as Ximinez, Gilliam as Fang, and the begoggled Jones as Cardinal Biggles – burst into incongruous settings, ('Nobody expects the Spanish Inquisition ...') and the first time attempted to torture Carol Cleveland with a dish-drying rack. Other joys included the Atilla the Hun Show, starring John as Atilla and Carol Cleveland as Mrs Atilla, and How to Recognize Different Parts of the Body. One of the most famous sketches was set in a shack in outback Australia, all the characters wearing bush hats with corks dangling from their brims and answering to the name of Bruce, and purporting to be the Philosophy Department of the University of Woolamaloo. Even such nonsense as this was pale in comparison with the *Python* versions of *Wuthering Heights* in semaphore, *Julius Caesar* on an Aldis lamp and

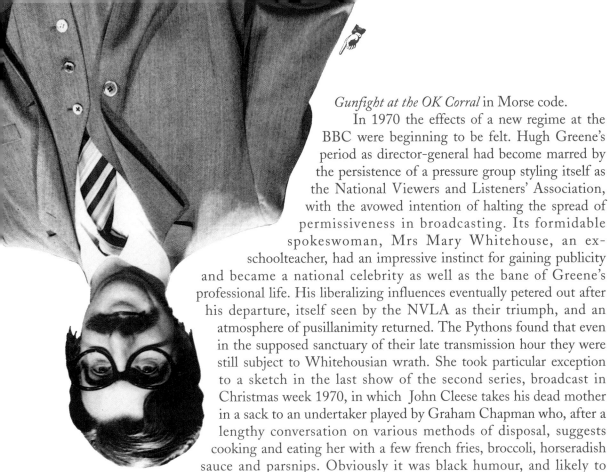

Gunfight at the OK Corral in Morse code.

In 1970 the effects of a new regime at the BBC were beginning to be felt. Hugh Greene's period as director-general had become marred by the persistence of a pressure group styling itself as the National Viewers and Listeners' Association, with the avowed intention of halting the spread of permissiveness in broadcasting. Its formidable spokeswoman, Mrs Mary Whitehouse, an ex-schoolteacher, had an impressive instinct for gaining publicity and became a national celebrity as well as the bane of Greene's professional life. His liberalizing influences eventually petered out after his departure, itself seen by the NVLA as their triumph, and an atmosphere of pusillanimity returned. The Pythons found that even in the supposed sanctuary of their late transmission hour they were still subject to Whitehousian wrath. She took particular exception to a sketch in the last show of the second series, broadcast in Christmas week 1970, in which John Cleese takes his dead mother in a sack to an undertaker played by Graham Chapman who, after a lengthy conversation on various methods of disposal, suggests cooking and eating her with a few french fries, broccoli, horseradish sauce and parsnips. Obviously it was black humour, and likely to offend those who were not on the appropriate wavelength. In fact, Terry Jones and Michael Palin doubted whether they could get away with it. After Ian McNaughton consulted Michael Mills, the head of comedy programmes, it was decided to let the item go ahead, with a somewhat contrived device of having the audience rush the stage at the climax to express disapproval, the chaos only brought to an end by the rolling credits and the playing of the national anthem. In repeats the sketch was eliminated altogether, although it has been performed in *Python* live shows.

'We were all very polite to one another during the first series,' recalled Michael Palin, 'we all submerged our idiosyncrasies for the general good of the show, but that wore off during the second series.' The Pythons' method of constructing them by reading out material to each other in a script meeting had its advantages and drawbacks, with a distinct edge in favour of Gilliam whose contributions were too obscure to cope with such exposure and had to be taken on trust, an arrangement that annoyed John Cleese most of all, because he felt that democracy was not being properly observed. 'As a general rule, the largest parts tended to be taken by people who had written them,' said Palin. 'How I could have written such an uncomfortable role as the Hermit, I'll never know.'

It was after the second series that the Pythons were signed up to make their first theatrical

ABOVE **A bewigged and moustachioed Idle**

131

film, the hastily produced *And Now for Something Complete Different* which was actually nothing of the sort, but merely a re-enactment of some of the more successful items from the first two series reshot on 35mm film in a widescreen format. For five weeks the team worked in various locations, with most of the interiors filmed in an improvised studio set up in a disused milk depot in North London. The Parrot Sketch, the Lumberjack Song in which a chorus of Canadian Mounties discover in successive verses that the rugged hero is a dainty transvestite, Pearl Harbor fought by the Townswomen in mud, the funniest joke in the world, killer cars, Hell's Grannies, the man with a tape recorder up his nose and the 'Upper Class Twit of the Year' contest were among the old favourites that were included. The film's producer, Victor Lownes, was then running the London Playboy Club, with its Hugh Hefner bunny-girls, which at that time was the most profitable of establishments in the Chicago-based empire on account of its gambling. Lownes intended to introduce the Pythons to a new audience in the United States, and he had high hopes for his film on the campus circuit. He asked, much to Terry Gilliam's annoyance, for a large credit to himself, carved out of stone, to be inserted in the middle of the title animation, and he also exercised a degree of creative control on which items should be included, leaving, as Palin put it, 'too many people sitting behind desks.' Although many of the sketches were given an extra gloss over their television originals, the final result was indigestible, a half-hour show stretched three times as long and without a plot, it was hard to retain the audience's attention span. The Pythons did not regard the experience with much pleasure and are annoyed when it is

compared with their subsequent films, which they were responsible for themselves.

'There were a number of very good performances,' said Palin, 'but unfortunately it doesn't expand on to the big screen very well. You can get away with very tatty sets on telly – it's all part of it – but you can't do the same apologies for quality on film.' Predictably, it was not the hoped-for success in America, as the Pythons were completely unknown to the audience at which the film was aimed, but because it was a low-budget work (the total cost was a ridiculously low £80,000) it was not difficult for it to go into profit on its British release. Inevitably, the group saw little of the financial returns themselves.

At least it brought home to the Pythons that they had an intrinsic commercial value as a group. The first series had been turned into a record album for the BBC but they were not entirely satisfied with the way in which it had been produced. So they established Python Productions as a means by which they could retain full artistic control of their various endeavours, and keep the profits. These included further albums and books. For Christmas 1971 *Monty Python's Big Red Book* was published, perversely with a vivid blue cover, its contents an assemblage of Pythonic absurdity adapted to the print medium, having been taken from the shows (a photostrip of Cleese doing a silly walk, the lyrics of the Lumberjack Song, a parody of the *Radio Times* commenting on the 'Upper Class Twit of the Year' contest, and so on) although the bulk of it was made up from original material put together by Eric Idle. A resourceful publisher, Geoffrey Strachan of Methuen, immediately perceived an excellent market for the book, and also helped to set up other spin-offs from television comedy shows, establishing a profitable explosion on the 'Humour' shelves in bookshops.

LEFT John Cleese regards Graham Chapman with some suspicion in the Half A Bee sketch

As far as *Monty Python* was concerned, following on the heels of the *Big Red Book* came *The Brand New Monty Python Bok*, a title that was to challenge newspaper typesetters – the paperback edition was *The Brand New Monty Python Pepperbok*. The bright white cover carried some very realistic inky thumb smears, causing consternation in bookshops where sales

staff and customers had failed to appreciate the joke. The second book, again compiled by Eric Idle, had rather less television-derived material, except for a picture-strip based on the *Salad Days* as directed by Sam Peckinpah, and was full of ingenious printing tricks, such as inserts and tip-ins, and a parody of a Penguin paperback.

Although there were voices in the BBC claiming it to be an inappropriate choice, the Corporation entry for the 1971 Montreux Television Festival was a *Monty Python* special put together from several of the shows, and it won the Silver Rose, an honour that clinched the third series. Lest that anyone should get over-excited, the BBC Handbook for 1972 merely mentions the award in a list of several other accolades received during the year by other programmes, with no other editorial reference.

Recordings for the third series began in December, although the first would not be on the air until the following October. Tensions were increasing within the team, with John Cleese, by now the most easily recognized member, also the most restless. He was often stopped in the street and asked to do a silly walk on the spot. It was not the fame, but the feeling of staleness that was affecting him, the sense that ideas were being regurgitated. 'I have an extremely low boredom threshold,' he admits. 'They wanted to hang on because they were enjoying it. I wanted to get away and do other things. I wasn't keen to do the third series, but I agreed to do seven, and was somehow pressured into doing thirteen, I found by that time we were repeating ourselves, and that the sketches we were writing were a combination of old ones. I could literally look at those sketches in the third series and say this item was a combination of this sketch from the first, and that from the second, with a twist on it. I wasn't getting much pleasure out of it.'

The other Pythons were uneasy and unimpressed by his increasing twitchiness. Recalling their reaction, Cleese says: 'The ones who were most vitriolic – and a couple were very rude about it, although I didn't realize it for a time – were the ones who were most threatened, because they weren't confident that they could earn a living outside the group. They were Terry Jones and Graham. Michael was the nearest to me in many ways – I don't think he was that bothered by the thought, and was happy to go off, but probably didn't feel quite confident enough to. And I think that Eric wasn't all that bothered, either – I think he felt like

BELOW **The Tudor Job Agency becomes involved in pornography smuggling...**

taking a risk. But Terry Jones has always felt frightened at operating outside the group – yet he's got masses of talent, masses.'

In corroboration Terry Jones agrees that in 1973 he did have a feeling that he had less going on outside *Python* than some of the others, and was the one who was most unhappy at the departure of John. 'I don't think I was vitriolic, though. I understood why John wanted to go. It's true that we had all thrown a lot into *Python*, but I don't think I was as angry as John imagines.'

Another factor affected the third series. Some sections of the BBC audience were finding *Monty Python* offensive. Organized pressure groups such as Mrs Whitehouse's National Viewers and Listeners' Association and the Festival of Light made a point of constantly lobbying the BBC's newly-appointed chairman, Lord Hill. Formerly a regular broadcaster known as the Radio Doctor, Hill had been switched from a similar position at ITV as a blatant

ABOVE **... Michael Palin, a modern police inspector, attempts to make a raid but turns into Sir Philip Sydney**

135

act of revenge by the Prime Minister, Harold Wilson, enraged by what he perceived as an unfriendly attitude on the part of the BBC towards his government. He had seen Hugh Greene off as director-general, one of the main sources of annoyance to the oppressors. Wilson's Labour government was defeated in the 1970 general election by Edward Heath and the Conservatives. Heath, however, saw no reason to remove Hill, who had been a Conservative Member of Parliament.

During the third series the Pythons found themselves for the first time subjected to the serious threat of censorship. 'We had been very spoiled,' says Michael Palin, 'and we had really done what we liked.' They had even generated a following in Germany, having made one show for Bavarian television in which they had spoken their lines phonetically, their outlandish accents adding to the audience's pleasure. Their second German show was to be a compilation of items from the BBC shows, but the Pythons were lukewarm and offered a counter proposal to stage a complete programme directed by Ian McNaughton in the Munich studios. McNaughton was somewhat astonished to receive a letter listing 'Thirty-two points of worry' which was based on an examination of all the programmes by Bill Cotton, the head of light entertainment, and Duncan Wood, the head of comedy. On his return from Germany McNaughton and the Pythons attended a solemn meeting at which they were told that words like 'masturbation' were not to be used in comedy shows. They were somewhat amused to note that a few of the objections were so fatuous that they revealed more about the objectors than anything else. Their would-be censors were, it seemed, unable to tell the difference between a severed arm and a giant penis. Cuts were made, but on a lesser scale than originally proposed.

BELOW John Cleese expertly demonstrates the complete silly walk

136

One of the sketches that had caused problems was the *All-England Summarize Proust Competition*, a spoof television quiz show in which the contestants were supposed to offer fifteen-second synopses of all the novels that formed *A la Récherche du Temps Perdu*. When it was the turn of Graham Chapman's character to be asked his hobbies he answered: 'Golf, strangling animals and masturbation,' but the BBC removed the last word from the audio track although lip-readers would not have been deceived. Arguments that the transmission time was so late that all those susceptible to corruption would have been safely tucked up in bed were unavailing.

There was, of course, a fundamental misunderstanding as to what the Pythons were attempting to do, by using shock effects such as severed limbs and simulated rape to extend the bounds of humour, which was far removed from the plain smut of stand-up comics in men's clubs. There was a certain irony in that they were making comments on, and mocking, the very permissiveness which they were seen to be promoting. Sketches such as Pasolini's *Third Test Match* in which naked lovers impede the bowling, and in the same programme those aimed at Oscar Wilde, wife-swapping and dirty vicars, cover the entire spectrum of Sunday newspaper-reading with devastating wit and sharp observation. George Harrison, the former Beatle, a *Python* devotee and a particular friend of Eric and Michael, says: 'Let's face it. There are certain things in life which make life worth living, and one of those things is *Python*. Especially to someone like me. When you've gone through so much in life, and you're supposed to decide what is real and what isn't, you watch the television and you see all this madness going on, and everyone is being serious and accepting it, and you're ready to bang your head on the wall in despair – then someone says, "And now for something completely

different!" That saves the day. Laughter is the great release.'

Much to the relief of the group, their second Munich show was made in English and later dubbed. The BBC showed it with the title *Monty Pythons fliegende Zirkus* and with the subtitle *Schnapps with Everything* in October 1973. In that same year the Pythons began a stage tour that took them around British cities for one-night performances. John, although unprepared to appear in any more television programmes, was happy to go on stage in live performance with the others. Neil Innes, Eric Idle's collaborator on *The Rutles*, also appeared with them. They followed their United Kingdom tour by accepting an offer to appear in Canada, but rapidly became aware of the vastness of the country, and they found the going much tougher with the venues at which they would appear ranging from huge city arenas to tiny basement clubs. They were also now fully aware of John Cleese's firm decision to do no more television with the group.

On their return to London they played for a season at the Theatre Royal, Drury Lane, a large auditorium normally associated with long-running, expensive musicals either imported from Broadway or due to be sent in the reverse direction. John could not be budged where television was concerned, placing the others in a difficult position, because the BBC was putting pressure on the Pythons for a fourth series. After long discussions it was decided that the series would go ahead without him, but that it would consist of only six shows instead of the customary thirteen, and that a subtle alteration of its title would occur in order to indicate subtly that a change had been made, namely the elimination of the words 'Flying Circus'.

'The group accepted my decision,' said Cleese. 'At least on the surface. And they went off and did their six shows, and they didn't apparently enjoy them that much. They didn't tell me immediately because it would have tended to confirm what I was already saying about doing more television. The shows were generally felt not to be as good as the first three series. I didn't actually think that. I didn't

see all of them – I saw three, but I thought that two were every bit as good. But there seems to be a received opinion that they weren't as good.'

There was however no longer the fine balance within the group, and its members felt jaded, finding ideas more difficult to come by. The Pythons had managed to achieve a remarkably coherent strength without having a natural leader – a true team in effect. It had worked because of its instinctive polarizing. Chapman and Cleese, Jones and Palin, Idle and Gilliam as associates on each side. Cambridge supplied verbal, logical, literate humour, with the absurdism springing from commonplace situations. The confrontation sketches were usually Cambridge-inspired. John Cleese was brilliant at delivering crescendoes of invective with fluid eloquence. Oxford was stronger in visual humour, and displayed a much more free-ranging imagination. Terry Jones and Michael Palin both believe they worked harder, and were prepared to stay in cutting rooms all night if need be. 'I was actually far more interested in form than John thinks,' says Jones. He recalled the making of *Monty Python and the Holy Grail*, the first film that the Pythons were prepared to call their own. 'The Cambridge side said, "Let's put it in if it's funny." Mike and I had to work very hard to make sure that lines went in that developed the plot, even if they weren't all that funny.'

While there was no overall leader, each faction had its respective front person, Cleese on the one hand, Jones on the other. They were the ones who were most likely to be in direct opposition to each other. As the series continued the acrimony and arguments in script meetings intensified, and led eventually to John Cleese describing them with some disgust as 'Democracy gone mad.' Astonishingly, from such conflict some of the finest comedy ever seen on British television flowed, with never a hint to the viewer of the angst that had produced it, the bending of egos and the suppression of individuality for the common good. If anything, it came as something of a surprise that they could present such a harmonious front, or even respect each other. John Cleese elaborated: 'Terry Jones is a very dominant personality, and several of the group have said to me that when I

FAR LEFT Civil service uniform – bowler hat and pinstripe suit – for the Ministry of Silly Walks

BELOW The 'Summarize Proust' competition caused tremors within the BBC

SUMMARIZE PROUST COMPETIT

1972 SUMMARIZE PROUST COMPETITION

7 THE PAST RECAPTURED
6 THE SWEET CHEAR GONE
5 THE CAPTIVE
4 CITIES OF THE PLAIN
3 THE GUERMANTES WAY
2 WITHIN A BUDDING GROVE
1 SWANN'S WAY

was present Terry and I would lock horns, which kind of balanced us. But in the fourth series Terry dominated too much, and they felt that the balance of the group had gone. And also, my kind of input in the writing wasn't there. They used a bit of the material that Graham and I had written. But the balance of the group had changed. And after that they didn't want to do any more television, either.'

Terry Jones commented on the fourth series, in answer: 'We were really at great disadvantages when we did the fourth series. Not only had John gone, but whereas in the past we had always written the show well in advance, always giving us plenty of time for setting-up, rewriting, editing the film, recording the show, then choosing in which order they went out – we'd always have shot six of them before the series started, so that we could choose the funniest to begin with, but now we had no choice of order, as the series started almost immediately. And where before we used to shoot forty minutes to cut it back to thirty, thereby discarding ten minutes, this time as part of a BBC economy drive they insisted that we only shot what we intended to use. It meant that we had no leeway there either. As it turned out, the best shows of that series were the third and the sixth.'

The third show was indeed spectacularly different, and a *Python* classic. It included a sketch in which Eric played a wartime squadron leader whose account of an encounter with the enemy is delivered in banter so arcane that even his colleagues are completely mystified.

RIGHT Mr Pither's Cycling Tour was the first complete narrative in a Python series

'Bally Jerry pranged his kite right in the how's your father. Hairy blighter, dicky-birdied, feathered back on his Sammy, took a waspy, flipped over his Betty Harper's and caught the can in the Bertie.'

Having repeated this gibberish three times to the mystification of all present, the alert is sounded and a pilot, Michael Palin, bursts in and shouts:

'Bunch of monkeys on your ceiling, sir. Grab your egg and fours and let's get the bacon delivered.'

More incomprehension. Michael tries again:
'You know ... bally ten-penny ones

dropping in the custard ... Charlie Choppers chucking a handful.'

Still bewilderment prevails.

'Sausage squad up the blue end.'

'No, still don't get it.'

'Cabbage crates coming over the briny?'

'No.'

Then over stock footage of a German bombing raid a voice-over says:

'But by then it was too late. The first cabbage crates hit London on July 7th. That was just the beginning ...'

Later in the same programme a court martial takes place in which Eric Idle, now a soldier,

ABOVE Michael Palin makes his way through the British Consulate in Smolensk which has gone Chinese

141

is accused of trivializing the war by flicking the enemy with wet towels and wearing special gaiters. In another sketch Graham Chapman plays a father obsessed with word sounds which he classifies as 'woody' or 'tinny', while surrounded by his upper-middle class family who look as though they have stepped out of a Shaftesbury Avenue drawing-room comedy of the 1930s. This particular show ended with a Neil Innes song, the only original serious number ever included in the *Python* series, 'Where Does a Dream Begin?'

The final curtain for *Monty Python* on television came on 5 December 1974 with the sixth programme in the fourth series, and the forty-fifth to be broadcast since 5 October 1969. It included the finals of the Worst Family in Britain; with the Garibaldis of Droitwich, then the Fanshawe-Cholmleighs of Berkshire, and the winners, the Jodrells of Durham who are too disgusting to be seen. A strange party political broadcast for the Liberal Party merged into the Nine O'Clock News, or the *Python* conception of it, with an item on capital punishment being introduced to sport, with the electric chair for threatening a goalie, and the promise of an interview with Mrs Ursula Hitler, a Surrey housewife who revolutionized British bee-keeping in the 1930s.

That was the end. As John had predicted, the Pythons no longer wanted to do any more series. They mutually decided the time had come to move into fresh enterprises. They had learned that it was necessary to control their work as much as possible, if it was to be free of outside influence. Their albums (apart from the first which the BBC marketed) were produced by Charisma, bringing in a substantial income. With the last one that they made under the Charisma contract, intentionally called *Monty Python's Contractual Obligation Album* they managed to make it into the Top Twenty chart. To some extent their achievement was boosted by the decision of the Independent Television Companies Association, the body that regulated television advertising, to ban commercials for it on the grounds that its contents were offensive. They thus gained a great deal of publicity without the necessity of having to pay for it. More press attention was directed at it when John Denver, whose publishers had given permission for a song to be used, took grave exception on discovering that it was parodied and

ended with their singer being strangled. He sued for defamation, and the offending track was deleted from the album.

It was the cinema which seemed to offer the best opportunities. Their brush with Victor Lownes aside, the Pythons were aware that a film for theatrical release would give them the chance to develop their ideas more ambitiously. So in the year of the fourth television series, 1974, they entered a deal with the theatre producer Michael White, who had staged *Cambridge Circus* in the West End, and who was also interested in the possibilities of film. The intention was to make *Monty Python and the Holy Grail*, with a manageable budget. The Pythons were to be paid a mere £2,000 each for their services, but they would also have a percentage on the returns. White enlisted interest in the pop and rock business, persuading groups like Pink Floyd and Led Zeppelin to invest.

Said Terry Jones: 'We'd all been convinced that we'd make a lot of money out of *And Now for Something Completely Different* but it came to about a thousand pounds, if it was anything at all. We still wanted to make a film and about the time of the third series we started writing a screenplay. We'd liked an idea of Mike's about King Arthur, and our first version was a mixture of old and new, with the Holy Grail being found in Harrod's. Harrod's, of course, had got everything. Then we took a year off from it. I'd got very heavily into the

BELOW **A sombre group of Pythons look straight into the camera**

Middle Ages by then, and I thought it would be great to set it one period so that we could give it an overall look.'

Unhesitatingly, John Cleese participated, his bar on television appearances with the others not applying to theatrical film. He remembers that only about ten per cent of the original idea survived into the final draft.

Cleese had made an extremely wise decision: *Monty Python and the Holy Grail* turned out to be a staggering box-office success, and because its budget was a low one, the returns were extremely satisfying. The Pythons published a comprehensive book on its production, with early draft script, notes, the production scripts, Gilliam drawings, stills, and even the complete, audited financial statement of production costs right down to the details of how much was spent on wigs and props. The total expenditure was £229,575.

The locations chosen were in remote parts of the Scottish Highlands, which apart from their timelessness, were often breathtakingly beautiful, justifying the discomforts of filming there, which included almost perpetual rainfall. The device of medieval characters talking and acting in a modern manner, so common in Hollywood historical films, was taken to absurd limits as the quest for the Grail embraced encounters with various characters and obstacles, such as the Knights who say 'Ni!', the guard who doesn't hiccough but tries to get things straight, the killer bunny rabbit, the extraordinarily rude Frenchman, the Bridge of Death over the Gorge of Eternal Peril, the Black Beast of Aarrgghh and a three-headed knight. The budget did not

RIGHT **Michael Palin equips Mr Zambesi, Terry Jones, with an artificial brain**

run to horses, so scenes that called for the knights to be mounted were simulated to the sound of coconut shells on the soundtrack, a curious device that somehow, given the generally preposterous atmosphere, did not seem all that intrusive. The sequence that came to be one of the best-remembered is a duel fought between Arthur and a Black Knight for whom things go badly, as one after another all his limbs are chopped off. His spirit, however, remains indomitable, and with his torso still upright he shouts after his departing victor: 'Come back here and take what's coming to you. I'll bite your legs off.' At the conclusion of the film a modern police car bursts into the frame and Arthur and his knights are arrested, while an inspector puts his hand over the camera lens.

Directing the film fell to the two Terrys, who found it an ordeal. Hitherto, Ian McNaughton had been the target of criticism, now they found themselves on the receiving end. Said Terry Jones: 'I usually agree with Terry G, especially then. We had very similar ideas about things, a joint feeling. We talked about how we were going to divide it up. It got to be either certain scenes, or we alternated every other day. I enjoyed it but I think Terry found it a frustrating experience. The producer, Mark Forstatter, was always saying it's hopeless having two directors, you never know where you are, but I was a bit oblivious to it, I thought it worked well. But we had a loony schedule. On one occasion we produced ten minutes of cut film out of a single day's shooting.'

The release of *Monty Python and the Holy Grail* was a turning point for the Pythons. They now found that they had time to pursue their separate ideas and enterprises, bringing to fruition projects that had remained in cold storage while the television series were progressing. They also found that at last they had reasonable money in their pockets. 'We had made a good living by BBC standards after being

145

together for six years,' said John Cleese. 'I used to get £240 per show, and probably £150 for writing it – so for seven months I would make something like five or six thousand. Well, on that sort of money you don't think you're going to the West Indies for three weeks. *Grail* was put together the way we put the television shows together. But then, in 1975 we started getting our royalties on it.'

Away from the Pythons he created a comic masterpiece for the BBC, writing in association with his wife Connie Booth, from whom he had separated and would soon be divorced. They remained happily capable of a working relationship. He was the star of *Fawlty Towers* and Connie played a supporting role. Basil Fawlty, the proprietor of a small residential hotel in the south-western resort of Torquay, was a manic, insensitive bully who lived perpetually on the borderline of hysteria. His short-fused temper, crass impatience and narrow perceptions ensured that when an awkward situation arose it would, in his hands, quickly become disastrous. Basil's mood switches were instant, one second he could be smarmily obsequious, the next a screaming madman. Countering him was Prunella Scales as his imperturbable and contemptuous wife, Sybil, whose indifference to his tantrums only served to make them worse. Connie played Polly, the put-upon maid of all work whose general incompetence was excused by the fact that she was an art student on starvation pay. Andrew Sachs played Manuel, a Spanish waiter with an almost total lack of English, who was the constant target of Fawlty's verbal and physical assaults.

Cleese had based the character on a genuine prototype he had encountered while on

location filming an early *Python* show in Devon, and in a country cursed with far too many surly innkeepers he was astonished by a man so rude that when asked by a guest for the time of the next bus to Torquay flung the timetable at him and told him to look it up himself. He first used him as the basis for a character in one of the *Doctor* scripts for Humphrey Barclay, before expanding it into the two series of *Fawlty Towers*, the first in 1975, the second in 1979, each consisting of six episodes, Cleese taking the decision that to stretch it further would dilute its impact. It remains a classic of television comedy, although there were occasions when some viewers felt that it tipped over into bad taste. The BBC entered an episode in the Montreux Festival, selecting that in which Fawlty has the problem of coping with a dead

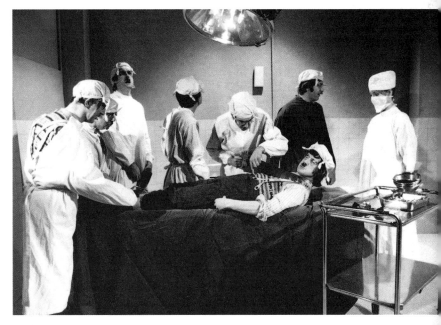

guest while at the same time catering for a visiting party of Germans. It did not go down well. Certainly its screening was handicapped by taking place at 9.00 am on a Sunday morning, with the sound not working properly. A huffy Swiss member of the audience observed that only the English found foreigners funny, and of course foreigners included the Swiss. Even so, *Fawlty Towers* was one of the BBC's best exported programmes. Books and scripts were published as spin-offs, but Cleese was not even prepared to allow a feature film.

In association with Anthony Jay he had started a company called Video Arts, which was

formed with the intention of producing training films for commerce and industry. Cleese's gifts were ideal for imparting boring information with enough wit and originality to make the message stick. Jay was previously a writer back in the days of *The Frost Report* and had become a notable theorist on the uses of television, having a strong belief that it had a potential far beyond mere entertainment. There was a certain irony in that Video Arts was not expected to make vast returns, but because it was in the vanguard of the video revolution it became enormously profitable, winning the Queen's Award for Exports in 1982, and providing Cleese with vast riches when his interest was eventually sold. He still continues to write and perform in some of their films, and he is, as a consequence of these, his feature films, and his appearances in television advertising, the most financially successful of the Pythons.

Eric Idle was, after John, the first Python to strike out on his own, creating for the BBC a comedy series called *Rutland Weekend Television*, which went to two series plus a Christmas special. From it was derived an ambitious spin-off, *All You Need is Cash*, starring the Rutles. The idea emerged from a bogus rock group in one of the RWT shows, called the Rutland Stones, for whom Neil Innes had written a parody musical number. As the guest host of NBC's comedy show *Saturday Night Live*, which goes out each week from the network's Rockefeller Center studios, he showed a clip but billed the group as The Rutles. Lorne Greene, executive producer of *SNL* and a dedicated follower of *Python* (there are many signs of *Python* influence in the American show) was sufficiently impressed to back a feature length mock-documentary on the lives of four Liverpudlian musicians whose lives bore a resemblance

to the real-life Beatles. Elaborating the joke was one of the original Fab Four, George Harrison, playing a music journalist in a sequence. Footage of real Beatles' incidents was spliced in, and Neil Innes composed several pastiche songs in appropriate Beatles idioms. The detail was painstaking; there was even an animation sequence to match the Beatles cartoon feature film *The Yellow Submarine*. In some respects the joke went too far, and the references were so obscure that only a dedicated Beatlemaniac would have understood them. As interest in the career of the 1960s supergroup seems to hold up more than thirty years since their first recording, Eric Idle's film has dated less than would be expected.

Terry Gilliam was anxious not to be regarded merely as a graphic designer, animator and cartoonist, and was drawn towards films. With Charles Alverson he wrote a screenplay, *Jabberwocky*, loosely based on the Lewis Carroll poem, and with the backing of Sandy Lieberson and John Goldstone it was turned into a film, with Michael Palin playing the lead, a cooper's apprentice mistaken for a prince who finds that he is expected to slay a horrible dragon-like monster that is spreading terror far and wide. Another Python, Terry Jones, appeared in it as a poacher. It was not, however, in any sense a *Python* film, but an entirely personal project of Gilliam's. All three – Gilliam, Palin and Jones – had a fascination for the Middle Ages. Gilliam perceived the times as being immensely filthy, and required his cast to engage in near-masochistic wallows in the

mud and worse. Tons of rubbish were strewn across the street set at Shepperton studios which had originally been built for the Dickensian musical *Oliver!*, and the actors were required to pick their way through the muck as though it was not there. The king, Bruno the Questionable, was played by the veteran comedian Max Wall without his teeth, and he was required to pick pieces of the crumbling palace ceiling from his food. A jousting scene in which tilting knights kill one another was filmed with the camera remaining fixed on the royal box in which the king and his retinue were drenched with showers of blood at each unseen encounter, until they were totally soaked. A double-page spread in colour of the final result caused readers of *The Sunday Times Magazine* to rise up in large numbers to protest, in spite of the fact that the 'blood' was the artificial concoction used in the film industry and commonly

FAR LEFT AND ABOVE
The Dirty Vicar Sketch:
Terry Jones as
Reverend Ronald Sims
who molests Carol
Cleveland

149

known as Kensington Gore.

The film's climax came about with an appearance of the Jabberwock itself, a hideous sauropod that looked like a manifestation of the imagination of Hieronymous Bosch or Gerald Scarfe. The critics were divided, some plainly uncomfortable in the presence of so much scatology, with dung and defecation jokes mingling unhealthily with severed limbs and buckets of blood. There was no question that the production design of Roy Smith and the cinematography of Terry Bedford had created a medieval atmosphere so vivid that it was almost possible to smell it.

Graham Chapman turned to films as well, becoming the co-producer and star of his own screenplay *The Odd Job*, with Peter Medak as the director. It was based on a television play by Bernard McKenna, about a man who was so much of a loser that he could not even expect to make a finished job of his own suicide, and so hires an odd-job man, David Jason, to carry it out for him. His circumstances change, and the need for such extreme action passes, but he finds that it is impossible to rescind the order. The film is a black comedy in which various people uninvolved in the main plot are killed as attempts to fulfil the contract are foiled and frustrated. It is possible that the film would have done better had it had a firmer release schedule. This had been a problem, almost from the beginning. Originally the lead, the David Jason character, was to be played by the eccentric rock star, Keith Moon of The Who, but by the time of shooting he was in hospital as a consequence of his chronic drinking, and would be dead within the year from a lethal mix of drugs and alcohol. Nor was Medak the first choice of director. It was to have been Cliff Owen, but he broke a thigh and had to be quickly replaced. In spite of the film's failure, which given its problem-filled gestation was not all that surprising, Graham continued to work with McKenna, and eventually they produced, with Peter Cook, the script for the pirate film which would become *Yellowbeard*.

Michael Palin appeared in a BBC film of Jerome K Jerome's *Three Men in a Boat* which was directed by Stephen Frears, before going on to play the lead in Terry Gilliam's *Jabberwocky*. In collaboration with Terry Jones he created the comedy television series *Ripping Yarns*, after a successful pilot, *Tomkinson's Schooldays*, directed by Terry Hughes, who had proposed the idea to them in the first place. A further eight films with varying subject matter were produced, the common theme being their tongue-in-cheek

homage to the Edwardian youthful adventure yarn.

Terry Jones had become a Chaucerian. 'Since about 1970 I had been beavering away on Chaucer in my spare time, and suddenly I found that I could take a year off to write my book. I've always felt that Chaucer was a good guy. What infuriates the academics is that I have studied him from the historical viewpoint, whereas they look at him purely as literature, and thus miss an enormous amount of what he is saying. When I've given talks at universities I have sensed their hostility.' The book he produced from his research, *Chaucer's Knight*, overturns the standard image of the 'verray, parfit, gentil knyght' and demonstrates that he was a bloodthirsty mercenary who roamed the eastern Mediterranean always ready to butcher for booty. It is not a dilettante's book but a formidable work of scholarship in a lucid and highly readable style, and apart from the appreciation of Chaucer it engenders, it has a fresh, imaginative approach that helps to counter the hackneyed and sterile teaching in many of

BELOW **John Cleese plays Dennis Moore, the highwayman notorious for stealing lupins**

Britain's schools which has the effect of destroying children's interest in the second greatest writer in the history of English literature (the first being Shakespeare). Given the lengthy time Terry Jones was working on the project there was little money in it for him, a factor that helped to endorse its credibility, but some academic critics were scornful of a comedian being allowed access to their sacred turf.

The Pythons, therefore, were all set up with interesting projects on which to work. At the same time they found that with the ending of the *Monty Python* series they had become national cult figures, their fame having spread to the United States. The first time they appeared on American television had turned out to be a dire experience. At the end of their Canadian tour they were guests on *Tonight* for NBC, where Joey Bishop

BELOW **The Hand of God points to Eric Idle in the Salvation Fuzz sketch**

was standing in as host instead of Johnny Carson. The audience was uncomprehending, never having heard of this bunch of British young men who wore drag and screeched at each other in idiotic female voices. Fortunately for the reputation of the Pythons, the Public Broadcasting Service had heard of them, being a major outlet for the BBC in the United States, and started running *Monty Python* shows, the first from KERA, the PBS station in Dallas, where the manager, Ron Devillier, was an enthusiast. They worked, in spite of fears that the shows would be regarded as too localized towards British audiences, with their constant mockery of the BBC logo and presentation techniques, which by American standards were peculiarly quaint. If anything it helped the Pythons achieve a following, particularly among viewers of college age. American students visiting Britain acquired *Python* albums and books and took them home, helping the group towards cult status. Soon PBS affiliates across the country were reporting that *Monty Python* was one of the most popular programmes in the schedules, and the American release of the theatrical film, *Monty Python and the Holy Grail* was found to be mutually helpful. Commercial stations started taking the *Monty Python* programmes on a local basis in some areas. The Pythons made a promotional tour for their film, leading to many television appearances, and one of the three main networks, ABC, decided that the time had come to join the circus.

BELOW Idle explains himself to the fuzz, Palin

Their flagship show aimed at a young audience and often given over to pop concerts, was ABC's *Wide World of Entertainment*. The network decided to make a bid for the whole of the Pythons' fourth series, made up of six half-hour shows, with the intention of running them together into two combined shows of three apiece. Unfortunately the BBC, being a non-commercial broadcasting organization, overlooked that in a ninety-minute time-slot on American television, allowance had to be made for twenty-four minutes of commercials, which would mean that it would be impossible to transmit the programmes in their original form as seen in Britain. Realization came too late. The first ABC transmission took place on 3 October 1975 at 11.30pm. It was not until the following month that Nancy Lewis, responsible for Python management in the United States, brought a videotape of the broadcast to London. The Pythons viewed it with horror. The cuts made for the insertion of commercials were crude and arbitrary, but far worse than that,

153

the programmes had been re-edited, with the sequences in a different order, key phrases had been removed, jokes bowdlerized to the point at which they ceased to make sense, and throughout the hand of the censor had been so heavily applied that Michael Palin commented that ABC had managed to make the BBC's censors look like pioneering liberals.

The second ABC compilation was due for transmission on the day after Christmas, 26 December. The Pythons urged the BBC to intervene, but the Corporation declined. They then asked ABC if they could be allowed to edit the programmes down to size themselves, but were given a firm refusal. After legal advice the Pythons then applied for an injunction in New York to stop the broadcast. They wanted a full hearing of their case, that the show going out with their names did not meet with their approval and was damaging to their reputation.

It fell to Terry Gilliam and Michael Palin to go to New York to present their case. ABC's lawyers gave them a list of the cuts that had been made, and then showed them the tape, which inevitably they found was unacceptable. Hopes of a settlement were dashed, and the next scenes were played out in the courtroom. ABC's attorney attempted to suggest that the Pythons were engaging in the action in order to publicize their live stage appearance in New York three weeks from then. His argument was unconvincing because he had managed to get an essential fact wrong, the Pythons were due to appear in four months, for a *three-week* run.

The full account of the court case, including *verbatim* exchanges taken from the official transcript of proceedings, is to be found in Chapter IV of the excellently documented, thorough and balanced book by Robert Hewison, published in 1981, *Monty Python: The Case Against*. The eventual outcome would turn out to have significance for all who wrote and performed their work on television.

The network's argument was that as they had the responsibility for protecting hundreds of television stations that ran their output, they had an absolute right to edit as they thought necessary. Commercial television in the United States, while capable of programming material of stupefying banality, has a tradition of exercising far more censorship than PBS, often as much to placate their sponsors and advertisers as to protect the viewing public. Certainly the whiff of hypocrisy was in the air.

BELOW **John Cleese about to make *the* announcement**

The judge, who had seen several Python shows and their *Holy Grail* film, was scrupulously fair, and accepted most of the Pythons' arguments. Palin and Gilliam had reined themselves in, in spite of occasional moments in the proceedings that were absurd enough to form part of a *Monty Python* sketch. He ruled, however, that an injunction served on ABC at that late stage would cause an unreasonable financial loss. He ordered that the broadcast could go ahead providing that it carried a disclaimer that it had been edited without the Python's approval, and that they wished to be dissociated from it. Unfortunately, ABC were able to go immediately to the Appeal Court where they won a stay of execution, and the airing went ahead with the words 'Edited for television by ABC', which were wholly unsatisfactory from the Pythons' point-of-view.

Luckily, the matter did not end there. The American legal system allows for plenty of reflection on decisions. The Pythons were able to appeal against the denial of an injunction, and after several months were able to prevent ABC from ever screening the shows again. What was particularly important was their ability to confirm that the copyright in the scripts was their own, and that a network had no right to alter or edit them without consent. The Pythons made history in copyright law in the United States by establishing an important precedent on the rights of an author over his or her output. They also accepted the copyright in their programmes outside the United Kingdom in lieu of damages, and the BBC was obliged to deliver to them the tapes of their forty-five shows, and the two ABC compilations. It meant that when the time came to issue the original programmes on video it was the Pythons, not BBC Enterprises, who would reap the rewards.

The Pythons, having enjoyed a period of working apart, decided that they ought to come together and make another film. The profits of the low-budget *Holy Grail* had fired their enthusiasm. The team (apart from Eric) was together again in 1976 for the one-night

LEFT **Palin entertains his audience**

155

Amnesty benefit, *Pleasure at Her Majesty's*, a monumental reunion of the Oxbridge wits – Alan Bennett, John Bird, Jonathan Lynn, Eleanor Bron, John Fortune, Jonathan Miller, Peter Cook, Bill Oddie, Dudley Moore, Tim Brooke-Taylor and Graeme Garden among them, and euphoria reigned. It was followed by the three-week appearance at the City Center, New York. During their earlier promotional tour in America for *Holy Grail* a reporter had asked what their next film was going to be. Eric immediately ad-libbed: *Jesus Christ – Lust for Glory'*.

The group started to talk about a new project in earnest, and kept returning to the biblical idea. To send up the good book was to embark on a rich field, hitherto untouched because of the problems of taste and taboo. It had not stopped Hollywood and particularly Cecil B DeMille in making turgid, overblown and, certainly for some, tasteless spectacles with religious themes. The Pythons began to think about a story which followed the life of an alternative Christ figure, and from that evolved the idea of basing it on an ordinary person who just happened to be around at Christ's big moments.

BELOW **The race for 'Upper Class Twit of the Year'**

LEFT **Palin and Cleese eye each other in the Parrot Sketch**

ABOVE *The Life of Brian:* Palin dances for Brian, Graham Chapman

Writing the script was not easy. Ideas were taken up with enthusiasm and later dumped in disgust. The Pythons' method of intense scrutiny of each member's material meant that a year passed before a reasonable first draft was put together, by which time *Brian of Nazareth* had begun to look possible. The next stage was to book a winter working holiday, without wives, girlfriends, children, agents and other personnel. Eric knowingly nominated Barbados as the place to go. Barry Spikings, then head of film production at EMI happened also to be staying on the West Indies island, and was intrigued to find the entire *Python* team taking up beach space. At that point their project was entirely speculative, the intention being to secure a deal when they had a finished screenplay. Spikings felt that it was one for EMI, and on returning to London immediately contacted the Pythons' producer, John Goldstone. After discussions, EMI agreed to back the film with a budget of $4.5 million, which put it in the major league compared with the paltry sum spent on *Holy Grail*.

Foreign locations were essential and now possible. Lord Grade had recently completed an ambitious mini-series, *Jesus of Nazareth*, which had been directed by Franco Zeffirelli. Many of the sets for it were still standing in Tunisia, at Sousse near Monastir and the two Terrys immediately flew off to look at them and to scout out the terrain which had a biblical look. Meanwhile production and costume design was put in train, along with other pre-production aspects, with shooting scheduled to begin in April 1978.

Again Mrs Mary Whitehouse, the national watchdog and self-appointed guardian of morals, crossed their paths. With her customary zeal and determination she brought a private prosecution for blasphemy against the newspaper *Gay News* and its editor, Denis Lemon, after a poem appeared that postulated a homosexual attraction between Christ on the Cross and a Roman centurion. Cases for blasphemy are extremely rare; this was the first since the 1920s, but it succeeded. Lemon was fined and given a suspended prison sentence. It was not just blasphemers, but the gay population who now appeared to be Whitehouse targets, a matter which deeply disturbed Graham Chapman who had not only co-founded and backed *Gay News* but was an active campaigner for the rights of homosexuals. The case went to appeal and although the suspended sentence was quashed the verdict was upheld.

The Pythons meanwhile were clocking up the bills for their film, with EMI's backing. They were under the impression that they would have sole artistic control. Barry Spikings was then informed by EMI's chief executive, Lord Delfont, that he was not only perturbed by the mounting costs, but that the Pythons could not have control. As the script stood it was impossible for Delfont to contemplate it being made. Clearly it was the possibility of a blasphemy prosecution that had upset him. Although a Jew he possessed what he regarded as a sacred obligation to the Christian patrons of his cinema circuit, the largest in Britain. Spikings had no option but to relay Delfont's decision to Goldstone that the film was cancelled.

BELOW **John Cleese diverts his soldiers between shots**

159

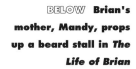

As a consequence the Pythons were very much out of pocket. EMI eventually paid over a small proportion of the expenses on the doomed project. Attempts were made to find other film companies prepared to rescue it, but it was hopeless. Then suddenly help came from an unexpected direction. George Harrison, the former Beatle, had as his business partner Denis O'Brien, a formidable figure in the financial world and a merchant banker who had worked for Rothschild's. Said Harrison: 'When I heard about the *Python* film, because they were friends of mine (especially Eric and Michael) and because I wanted to see their movie I had a word with Denis – "How can we help my mates?" And a little while later Denis rang me back and said "OK, I've figured a way to get it made," and he got it rolling.' It was the start of HandMade Films which for the next decade produced a number of interesting British films including *Time Bandits*, *A Private Function*, *The Long Good Friday* and *Withnail and I*.

The production was delayed by six months. The direction was solely in the hands of Terry Jones, with Terry Gilliam as the production designer. Each Python played several roles apiece, except the lead which fell to Graham, and the title became *Monty Python's Life of Brian*. Even when it was finally finished it went through several edits and test previews before being considered ready for the critics to see. They were, given the *Gay News* furore, at pains to ensure that no one could possibly conclude that it was a life of Christ. At the beginning of the film the three wise men burst into a Nazareth stable where the shrewish Mandy (Terry Jones) is giving birth. She exercises her tongue on them in spite of their lavish gifts, and they are nonplussed. It is only when they spot another stable down the road ablaze with bright lights do they realize that they have come to the wrong manger. Later there is a Sermon on the Mount scene where a distant Jesus is seen but is speaking too indistinctly to be heard on the fringes of the crowd. At the end there is a crucifixion, and Brian is indeed hanging on the cross, but he is just one of many suffering the same fate, with Eric Idle getting them all to join in his jaunty, upbeat

BELOW Brian's mother, Mandy, props up a beard stall in *The Life of Brian*

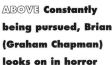

song on always looking on the bright side of life. The Romans used crucifixion as a common punishment and such mass executions occurred as a matter of historical fact. (Eric's song, for which he wrote both words and music, was dubbed, he remembered while he lay horizontal on the floor of a Tunisian hotel from half a bottle of Boukha. Thirteen years later, in 1991, it was number one in the ITV charts, number three in the BBC's. Gary Lineker, his neighbour and friend, was the first to tell him that the football terraces were singing it. After the disc jockey Simon Mayo played it every morning, Virgin were forced to release it as a single, and it shot up the charts.)

As in *Holy Grail* much of the humour in *Life of Brian* is dependent on the juxtaposition of modern ideas, attitudes and speech idioms with the historical setting. It is even more sophisticated than that. The People's Liberation Front of Judea, a terrorist organization that is plotting to kidnap Pilate's wife and carry out other acts intended to demoralize their Roman occupiers, conducts its meetings as though they have been convened by a group of trade union shop stewards. 'What have the Romans ever done for us?' complains their leader, John Cleese, before he grudgingly, but with an elaborate regard for fairness, accepts a lengthening list of improvements that have been brought about by the invaders, so that their eventual statement cannot be faulted for inaccuracy. Much is also made of the human psychology which causes people to believe what they want to believe, often in the face of logic. Brian spends much of the time being pursued by a mob who are convinced that he is the Messiah, even in the face of

ABOVE **Constantly being pursued, Brian (Graham Chapman) looks on in horror**

ABOVE **A relaxed Python team at the Tunisian location for** *The Life of Brian*

clear evidence that he is not.

When the film was released a small, highly vocal group, the Festival of Light, condemned it, unseen. The British Board of Film Censors (BBFC), a then voluntary body that had been set up many years earlier by the film industry in order to protect it from the scores of local authorities who were prepared to exercise the right of veto on anything playing in their areas, was unwilling to certify the film until legal views had been canvassed. Problems were occurring overseas as well. A radio programme about the making of *Life of Brian* was banned by CBC, the Canadian state-run national broadcasting organization, and the Pythons' shows were also dropped. CBC officials in Montreal faced a demonstration by McGill students dressed as Gumbies. (It is just possible that CBC loyalists had been offended by the Lumberjack Song in which a bunch of tough Mounties sing along with a transvestite woodcutter.) Methuen, the Pythons' publisher in England, now hesitated to proceed with the *Life of Brian* book that was in preparation.

Then in August 1979 the BBFC passed the film without cuts, giving it an AA certificate, restricting it to an audience of over-fourteens. In the same month it opened in the United States with an R rating, enabling it be shown to anyone under seventeen only if accompanied by an adult. The imprimatur of the BBFC was insufficient to prevent if from being picked off by various religious organizations and pressure groups. The Catholic Church condemned it, and made it a sin to attend screenings. There was even a pressure group formed called Citizens Against Blasphemy with the express intention of bringing a prosecution, which it failed to achieve. However, demonstrations and denunciations raged. An articulate right-wing columnist on the *New York Post*, William Buckley, actually wrote that Monty Python was crucified at the end of the film, a baroque leap of the imagination that had not even occurred to the team themselves. Not until the appearance of Martin Scorsese's serious film *The Last Temptation of Christ* in 1988 was so much hot air in the name of religion spouted on both sides of the Atlantic. When *Life of Brian* was

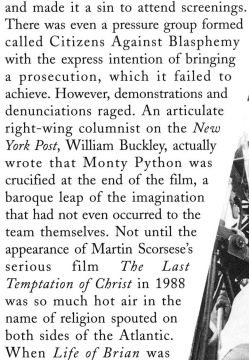

BELOW **A regal Pontius Pilate looks down on his director, Terry Jones**

released in America howls of rage were heard throughout the great Bible Belt, and in so many small towns in southern and south-western states were huge pressures directed against theatre owners, that the film was banned or cut-off in mid-run. Obviously, as is invariably the case, the outcry was good for the box-office, and in those places where it was allowed to be seen without interference it was a hit, and already in profit by the time of its London opening in November.

The Festival of Light adopted different tactics for their British campaign. They lobbied local authorities to exercise their statutory right to overturn the BBFC decision and ban the film outright in their areas. Local options have always been possible but are rarely exercised, except in one or two areas with a reputation for non-conformity. When *Life of Brian* opened in the West End, John Cleese and Michael Palin took part in *Friday Night, Saturday Morning*, a BBC talk show hosted by Tim Rice, and were savagely attacked by the Bishop of Southwark, Dr Mervyn Stockwood, and Malcolm Muggeridge, who had at least seen the film. A fierce and bitter argument developed in which Bishop Stockwood suggested that they were all getting the thirty pieces of silver for their work. Cleese protested that the film was really about closed minds that were not prepared to question faith and that it was not an attack on faith itself, but his point was ignored by the two ageing and voluble critics. As it was Tim Rice's first experience as a TV talk show host they made the most of it. 'I just left them to get on with it,' he said.

BELOW Idle, Cleese and Palin watch the shooting of the film

Not surprisingly, huge swathes of Britain banned the film and in other places its rating was upgraded to an X which kept the under-eighteens away altogether. One district council worked itself into such a lather of indignation in posting its ban that it was considered rather unsporting to point out that it actually had no cinema screens within its boundaries.

The Pythons were able to earn their thirty pieces of silver and more besides. The notoriety undoubtedly helped the box-office chances, although until Rupert Murdoch came along with BSkyB it was kept off television. Even among the Pythons themselves, *Life of Brian* is regarded as the apotheosis of their film work.

The next joint celluloid venture was more straightforward. In 1980 they played for four nights at the Hollywood Bowl before an audience of 8,000

dedicated followers, deliberately making only half of the vast amphitheatre available, since at full capacity it would have been hard for the furthermost sections of the crowd to see anything. The fans greeted each number, the Parrot Sketch, the Four Yorkshiremen, the Lumberjack Song, the Custard Pie Sketch, the Singing Waiters and many others with frenzied applause, very much in the way that a Las Vegas audience bursts into applause as soon as Sinatra starts in on a popular favourite such as 'Strangers in the Night'. The Pythons were relaxed, confident and mellowing. John Cleese walked up and down the aisles with a vending tray, hawking 'Albatross, live albatross'. Graham Chapman performed his celebrated one-man wrestling. The other significant outcome at the time was John's first meeting with his second American wife, Barbara Trentham. As she put it: 'It was mild curiosity at first sight.'

A feature film was made of the event, edited together from the four nights and assembled in a different sequence. *Monty Python Live at the Hollywood Bowl* did not have much of a cinema release, but remains a popular seller on video, an anthology of *Python Golden Hits* played out in the Californian sunshine.

The Pythons as individuals were also continuing to churn out books. Graham's autobiography, a baffling mixture of truth and absurdity, appeared as *A Liar's Autobiography Volume VI*. Terry Gilliam produced *Animations of Mortality*, an account of his graphic methods, which used illustrations from many of his *Monty Python* animated sequences. Terry Jones, having seen his *magnum opus*, *Chaucer's Knight* into print, followed with a collection of fairy tales, illustrated by Michael Foreman. The text of Eric Idle's play *Pass the Butler* was put into book form, in spite of its disappointingly short life in the West End. Michael Palin turned his attention to the screenplay of *Time Bandits* which he wrote with Terry Gilliam for HandMade. The story was of huge appeal to children, although it was not intended to be a juvenile film. The bandits in the title were a motley crew of picaresque dwarfs who, having stolen a precious map of the universe, can roam through any era at will. They burst into the suburban bedroom of a young lad, Kevin, and whisk him off to meet Robin Hood (John

LEFT AND BELOW
Palin judges Brian who the mob believes is The Messiah

Cleese), Agamemnon (Sean Connery) and Napoleon (Ian Holm). The nature of the adventure's onset is appealing, when a knight in full armour suddenly emerges through the wall of Kevin's bedroom, like a particularly vivid dream. The dwarfs are rambunctious, quarrelsome, assertive and competitive, each a perfectly formed character with unique idiosyncrasies. Robert Hewison observed that they were not unlike the Pythons, in fact. My son, then aged four, rather startled Terry Gilliam after a Sunday morning preview by declaring that it was like *The Wizard of Oz*. True, it was, but it needed a child's imagination to notice it, particularly as young minds are more appreciative of hard-edged fantasy than adults. *Time Bandits* was not particularly successful in Britain, but in America it was a hit, and not only made money for Gilliam but furthered his directing reputation, demonstrating the fecundity of his cinematic imagination.

After *Time Bandits* Michael Palin, who appeared in a relatively small part, wrote another film for HandMade. *The Missionary* set out to expose the double standards that held together life in Edwardian England, the hypocrisies of class and manners, and the resigned toleration of a grotesque underclass by those who ruled society. Palin played a clerical exile returned from Africa who is prevailed upon by his bishop to look after fallen women in the East End. The cinematography of *The Missionary* is impressive, with fine compositions rendered in soft, misty colours like late Victorian and Edwardian genre paintings. Michael Palin has a theory that comedy works better if it also looks good.

There was still time for a last *Python*

BELOW Palin, Rowan Atkinson, Cleese and Jones sharing an after-dinner joke in *The Secret Policeman's Ball*

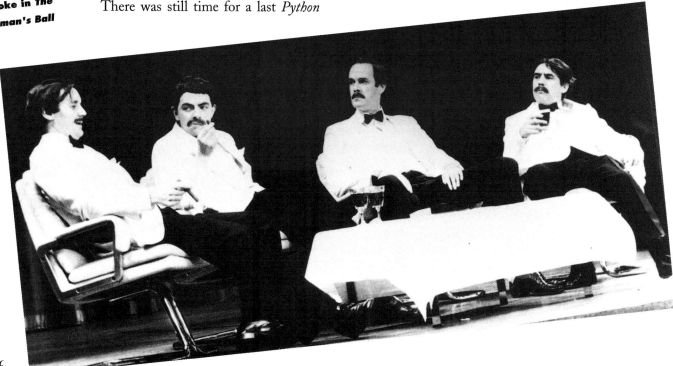

film. The group enjoyed its occasional get-togethers and felt that another movie should be made. It emerged as *Monty Python's The Meaning of Life*, something of an all-embracing title, which left the way open for a broad range of ideas. For months the struggle went on to create a coherent screenplay, but at some point a decision was taken to drop any thought of a continuous narrative, and instead to concoct a series of large self-contained sketches, each of which would illustrate the seven ages of man, from birth through to his visitation from the Grim Reaper, with a subsequent peek at the hereafter. Once again the final draft was hammered out in the sun-drenched Caribbean, in this case Jamaica. Terry Jones was designated director, with the other Terry in charge of what was called The Other Unit. A

LEFT **Pamela Stephenson and John Cleese in *The Secret Policeman's Other Ball*. The policeman, Graham Chapman, is also about to strip**

deal was made with a Hollywood major, Universal, allowing the Pythons the freedom they asked for. Denis O'Brien was disappointed, believing that with successful marketing techniques he could have made each Python a substantial multi-millionaire, but his plans had not been appreciated.

Said Michael Palin: 'The Pythons don't like being leant on. The more we're leaned on the more we bridle. The BBC tried it. ABC wanted to make us stars of their network, we sued to be taken off. Whenever heavy commercial pressures are put on the Pythons we always react against it. Denis, with the best will in the world, tried to line us up with big corporations in America to sell our material – we were offered shares in companies and that kind of thing – and for a month it all looked wonderful. Then we all looked at each other and said, "This is not our world – we're not really happy here." End of Python International Inc. Back to our little office and all the people we've worked with before.'

At the start of *The Meaning of Life* the Pythons appeared as fish, demonstrating the evolutionary nature of man. 'The fish costumes were dreadful,' complained John in his

167

ABOVE **Idle and Palin as disrobed judges in *Monty Python Live At the Hollywood Bowl*, 1982**

traditional role of chief whinger. For him the filming was its usual chaotic and uncomfortable experience. For Terry Jones it went like a dream. It was shown to small groups at Christmas 1982 and as a consequence several changes were made, the most drastic being the removal of the Terry Gilliam sequence from the body of the film to its own special place as an attached featurette preceding it. In the initial stages Gilliam had been reluctant to return to animation, but given a huge budget found the challenge suddenly irresistible, and was able to produce some of his finest work. He also designed the main title in a Pythonic idiom. *The Meaning of Life* was a portmanteau work, a pot-pourri with something to offend everyone. In one of the best sequences Michael Palin plays a gritty northern worker who returns home to his grim terrace having been made redundant and faces a horde of children procreated as a consequence of his refusal as a good Catholic to consider contraception. His announcement that they will all have to be sold for medical experiments leads to a huge production number that flows into the cobbled alleyways, involving unemployed workers, street urchins, housewives, cardinals, nuns throwing up their heels to

BELOW **A reprise of the hugely popular Lumberjack Song**

Palin's song 'Every Sperm is Sacred.' In another sequence of the film John Cleese plays a master in a public school teaching his extremely bored class the practical aspects of sex, using his wife as a demonstrator. The boys behave with as much studied indifference as if the subject had been irregular Latin verbs.

The most revolting sketch had Jones as the balloon-like Mr Creosote, the grossest of all gluttons, dining in an expensive restaurant and vomiting frequently into a bucket provided by the obsequious head waiter, Cleese. Eventually the disgusting creature, having taken one titbit too many, explodes and showers the entire restaurant with regurgitated debris. The vegetable soup that was used to simulate the vomit began to acquire lifelike characteristics after three days' filming, adding further weight to Cleesian complaints.

In June 1983 *The Meaning of Life* opened in London, following a successful run in the United States. At the Cannes Film Festival it was a British competition entry and to the astonishment of the Pythons, and even a few film critics, was awarded the Special Jury Prize,

the second highest honour on offer. Reflecting on it in 1994 Eric Idle said: 'It was only one rewrite short of a great film. If only we had gone back and put the seven ages of man over *The Meaning of Life* we could have avoided all those captions and followed the story of one character, jumping though history, as he ages. I know, now he tells us.'

It was the last time all of the Pythons were together in one film. Three of them were to appear in *Yellowbeard*, the pirate comedy written by Graham Chapman that he had spent several years trying to get off the ground. He was joined by Eric and John together with a formidable team of comedians, including Peter Cook, Cheech and Chong, Madeline Kahn and Marty Feldman, who died during the filming. It was not a success.

John Cleese's career progressed in a number of interesting ways. He played a bone-headed English army major in charge of a bunch of camp, in every sense, entertainers in Malaysia after the war, in the film of Peter Nichols' stage play *Privates on Parade*, directed by Michael Blakemore. It was a project that Denis O'Brien had hoped would feature all of the Pythons, but they declined. Most people connected with the production lacked film experience, and it failed to match the impact of the play.

For some years John had been in therapy, having begun when his first marriage was breaking up, and he found it of great benefit. So impressed was he, in fact, that he decided to pass on some of the things he had learned, and with his therapist, Robin Skynner, he concocted a book of dialogues called *Families and How to Survive Them* which, because of its easily-assimilated tone, attracted a large readership and has remained a consistent bestseller. In 1993 they published a sequel, *Life and How to Survive It*.

In 1985, taking off in another direction Cleese appeared in *Silverado*, a Hollywood western co-written and directed by Lawrence Kasdan, playing a British sheriff, with Kevin Kline, Kevin Costner, Scott Glenn and Danny Glover as cowboys. The idea of a sheriff with an English accent was not historically inaccurate; many immigrants had become lawmen in the pioneer days. Cleese learned to ride for the film, and was disappointed that most of the

time he was on a horse he is in the distance and out of focus. It was followed by *Clockwise*, directed by Christopher Morahan from a screenplay by Michael Frayn, a comedy in which he plays a pompous comprehensive-school headmaster who runs his life to a precise time-table. Invited to chair the Headmasters' Conference, normally confined to the independent schools, he fails to get on the right train, attempts an alternative means of getting there, and more or less destroys his life in the course of one day. It was well-received in Britain, but its humour did not survive the Atlantic crossing where, for instance, the concept of an entire row of non-working payphones was entirely alien.

Cleese was able to put much that he learned from the experience to use in *A Fish Called Wanda*. The director was Charles Crichton, who had been responsible for some of the short films made by Video Arts, and was the veteran of classic Ealing comedies such as *Hue and Cry*, *The Lavender Hill Mob* and *The Titfield Thunderbolt*, and part of the cleverness of the film's appeal was that two of the leading members of the cast, Kevin Kline and Jamie Lee Curtis, were American. They play Otto and Wanda, a pair of crooks visiting London for a jewel heist carried out in conjunction with an English gang that includes Michael Palin as Ken, a stuttering animal-lover. John Cleese cast himself as Archie, a stuffy barrister whose outlook is suddenly broadened by the disastrous eruption of Wanda into his life. It was the first film on which he had worked where Cleese had managed to have a say in the logistics, and consequently he found the experience generally satisfying. One of the funniest scenes, depending on split-second timing, took place in Archie's home, where he finds himself first entertaining Wanda who has let herself in, then coping with the jealous Otto, then trying to explain to his drab, but deeply suspicious

171

wife Wendy, Maria Aitken, who unexpectedly returns, just what is going on.

The American success of *A Fish Called Wanda* led to immediate calls for a sequel which at first Cleese resisted, but there is one now in the early pre-production stages. Meanwhile he continues to appear in other films, most recently in *Mary Shelley's Frankenstein*, directed by Kenneth Branagh, and the new live-action version by Disney of *The Jungle Book*, directed by Stephen Sommers.

Michael Palin has maintained fairly consistent multiple careers as an actor, writer, television documentarist and latterly playwright. He played the lead in *A Private Function*, a film written by Alan Bennett, and directed by Malcolm Mowbray which was set in a Yorkshire town in 1947, the year of the wedding of Princess (now Queen) Elizabeth and Prince Philip, and the peak of British rationing, which was actually more acute then than it had been during the war. The attraction for Palin was the opportunity to act again with Maggie Smith, who had enlivened *The Missionary*. Terry Gilliam next cast him against type in *Brazil*, his bleak view of a future Britain. Palin played a sadistic government interrogator, the first time that he had been allowed to get his teeth into an unsympathetic character. His most interesting appearance to date has been in the gentle romance, *American Friends*, based on a memoir by a Palin ancestor. Palin co-wrote the screenplay with Tristram Powell, who also directed in

picturesque locations such as Oxford and Switzerland, and his co-stars were Trini Alvarado and Connie Booth, who played the girl's chaperone. In spite of the obvious attractions the film, gratefully received in Britain as a relief from the mindless violence that is the normal cinema diet of the 1990s, has not been shown properly in the United States.

Palin has latterly become a national figure as a consequence of his globe-hopping television series, *Around the World in 80 Days* and *Pole to Pole* for the BBC. His easy, spontaneous style attracted high ratings, and carved out a new public that may never have connected him to the Pythons, as well as spawning a couple of bestselling books. In 1994 he made a further series, this time getting no further than the Isle of Wight which he attempted to examine from his position as a local journalist.

Terry Gilliam, his credentials as a film director enhanced by the success of *Time Bandits* in the United States, began writing his post-Orwellian vision of the future, *Brazil*, in collaboration with the playwright Tom Stoppard, whom he found had an idiosyncratic method of working. As the script slowly evolved, Gilliam worked out a way of describing the plot to curious journalists. It was, he

MONTY PYTHON

said: 'Walter Mitty meeting Franz Kafka.' Why the strange title? 'The song "Brazil" is a sort of kitsch samba number popular in the Forties, the sort of thing people would hum to keep their spirits up in tough times, suggesting escape into an exotic dream world of blue seas, waving palms and golden beaches.' He described the setting for his film as 'somewhere on the Belfast-Los Angeles border'.

The leading figure in the film is played by Jonathan Pryce, a clerk in a Ministry of Information basement, surrounded by heating ducts and primitive-looking computer equipment. A bug, quite literally, gets into the system, and the file on a terrorist, played as an urban-guerilla heating engineer by Robert De Niro in a balaclava hood, a cigar permanently in

ABOVE **Graham Chapman is chased to his dream death**

173

his mouth, is altered, saving him from arrest. In checking the mistake Pryce encounters his dream girl, Kim Greist, and realizes that escape from the bureaucratic monolithic existence to which the population is condemned is actually possible.

The ambitiousness of *Brazil* proved a handicap to its appeal. A long film, 142 minutes, it was initially shelved by its American distributors who found in particular that the trick ending, which seems to be a happy one, but is dramatically revealed to be quite the opposite was unacceptable and demanded that it be changed, thus in Gilliam's view totally destroying the integrity of the film. Gilliam campaigned, and the Los Angeles film critics having seen it, gave it awards for best picture, best director, best screenplay, without it even being released. A stand-off resulted, and when it was finally broken, Universal rushed the film out to qualify for the Academy Awards (it gained two nominations but no Oscars). Finally released, it died, unappreciated by audiences and unsupported by the advertising necessary to get it accepted in American cinemas.

If the experience of *Brazil* was traumatic, Gilliam's next film was a monumental fiasco, although he was not the culpable party. *The Adventures of Baron Munchausen* was a project that had long interested him. The film was shot in Rome, and with a budget of $46 million proved to be the most expensive film ever made there since Darryl F Zanuck's monumental *Cleopatra*, an unfortunate precedent. John Neville was cast as the eighteenth-century Baron, with supporting parts played by Eric Idle, his faithful servant and the fastest man in the world who could run to Spain and back in an hour to fetch a bottle of wine, Oliver Reed as the god Vulcan, Robin Williams as

BELOW Terry Jones receives presents from his platoon as they prepare to go over the top

the fast-talking Moon King (uncredited and seen as a giant head detached from its body), Valentina Cortese as his queen, Uma Thurman as Venus, and Sarah Polley as Munchausen's ten-year-old companion on his trips into the crater of Etna, Vulcan's forge in the centre of the earth, the Moon and other stopovers in the Baron's fantastic odyssey.

Production troubles abounded. 'It was the best of times, it was the worst of times,' said Eric Idle. 'Not since the First World War have British boys been put through so much abroad. I had my head totally shaved for six months.' The German producer, Thomas Schüly, rapidly went into isolation. Said Gilliam: 'We hardly spoke after the first week. He was too busy giving interviews and being photographed with his muscle-building equipment.'

Gilliam's film was swept up in the politics surrounding David Puttnam's abrupt departure as production head of Columbia in Hollywood, and failed at the box office, never having a hope of recouping the money it cost. It is a breathtaking work, jammed with exciting, innovative cinematic ideas, and should be a film future generations will marvel at.

Gilliam inherited his next film, *The Fisher King*, and turned it into something interesting. A late-night radio host, Jeff Bridges, inadvertently goads a psychotic listener into the massacre of a restaurant full of people, and in remorse gives up his career. A couple of years later and close to the skids, he meets a mystic, played by Robin Williams, through whom Bridges achieves redemption.

Terry Jones also pursued a post-Python film career. For Jim Henson, the Muppets'

LEFT **Graham Chapman gives some very precise instructions in *The Meaning of Life***

175

creator, he wrote *Labyrinth*, a fantasy in which Jennifer Connelly has to enter another world, rather as Alice went through the looking-glass, in order to save her baby brother from the clutches of the king of the goblins, played by David Bowie, an ordeal that takes her into a series of adventures and encounters with curious creatures. They sprang from the fertile imagination of the designer, Brian Froud, and he and Jones later published a book of them.

He next directed *Personal Services*, which was written by David Leland and based on the story of Cynthia Payne, a well-intentioned woman who set up a discreet brothel in Streatham catering for the eccentric tastes of a clientele that included judges, senior civil servants and other outwardly respectable figures. It was broken up in heavy-handed police action and the lady went to prison. The character based on Payne is played by Julie Walters, a comic actress with the capability of shading a role. She makes her both assertive and tenderly vulnerable, and Jones' film treats her customers with sympathy, without mocking their bizarre predilections. In a sense *Personal Services* is an insightful documentation of an aspect of British social behaviour that is rarely covered in the cinema because it is generally inseparable from prurient interest. The film was moderately successful in Britain, but not in America where a personnel change at the top of its distributing company helped to have it buried.

ABOVE ... which ends up on the cleaning woman's head

Jones had written a children's book called *Erik the Viking* and in 1989 a film of that title was released, written and directed by him, and in which he took the part of an eccentric island king. The book was a collection of stories, but the film is an original. Erik, played by the American actor Tim Robbins, lives in a Norse village on the edge of a fjord and he becomes fed-up with the constant persecution by John Cleese's villainous tyrant. Erik learns that the only way to stop this is to bring back and blow the Horn Resounding from the island of Hy-Brasil which lies beyond the Gates of the World. An interesting cast (Eartha Kitt as a soothsaying hag, Imogen Stubbs as a demure princess, Antony Sher as a weapons-maker with a vested interest in continued persecution) moves the action along in an imaginative fashion, but Jones was angered that the final cut was not his, and the version released in Britain and America suffered from the inclusion of unsatisfactory footage which he had excised. He later directed one of

the segments of *Young Indiana Jones* for George Lucas, set in Spain in 1917. For Lucas he was willing to direct for television, and it meshed perfectly with his own projects in preparation.

Eric Idle regards one of the highlights of his post-Python career as his two seasons in 1987 with the English National Opera singing Ko-Ko in Jonathan Miller's production of *The Mikado* (which in 1989 was staged again in Houston). 'Fun and fabulous,' he said, 'and a chance to work with Jonathan, one of my early heroes.'

Idle has concentrated on writing and performing, confining directing to an episode of Faerie Tale Theatre, *The Frog Prince*, which starred Robin Williams and Teri Garr. He has also attempted producing, commissioning Gary Sinyor to write *Leon the Pig Farmer*, an inventive British comedy which Sinyor and his co-director Vadim Jean later set up themselves after a rejection from Universal. Of many film performances the most satisfying was *Nuns on the Run*, directed in 1990 by his old Footlight chum Jonathan Lynn ('We bought our first leather jackets together at Cambridge') which co-starred Robbie Coltrane as a fellow small time crook forced with him to take refuge in a convent ruled by a puzzled Janet Suzman. 'Happiness', said Eric.

He executive-produced and appeared in *Splitting Heirs* directed by Robert Young from Eric's screenplay, which was the 1993 official British entry at Cannes. A variant of the *Kind Hearts and Coronets* theme, Eric played a changeling who discovers too late that the dukedom he should have inherited has gone to a vulgar American, Rick Moranis, and is persuaded by a shady lawyer, John Cleese, to bump him off, which means first getting past the nymphomaniac dowager duchess played by Barbara Hershey. The critics were unkind. 'You wouldn't think, talking to Alexander Walker, that they wanted a British film industry, given the speed at which they slag off your work,' said Eric.

More recently he has appeared as what he describes as 'a naff villain, a sort of elderly toy boy of Kathy Moriarty' in Steven Spielberg's production of *Casper the Friendly Ghost*. Rumours suddenly erupted, prompted by a supposed *Mail on Sunday* scoop, that he was to play Dr Who,

Spielberg having bought the rights to the vintage BBC time-travelling series. The announcement turned out to be premature as the idea still had not been sold to a television network, and Eric was one of several possible candidates to pilot the Tardis. That he would make a good choice there can be no doubt.

The Pythons came together for the last time in 1989, to appear in a sketch for a programme celebrating their twentieth anniversary, with Steve Martin. Graham Chapman was then terminally ill with cancer but was brought from hospital to be with them in what turned out to be a very emotional occasion in which many people who had worked with the Pythons over the years came to see him. In the end the sketch was not used although there were glimpses of Graham in the final cut. The cancer had been diagnosed in his throat nearly a year earlier and he had undergone treatment, although it spread to his spine. He achieved a remission and was planning new projects, but in September it was found that his condition was hopeless. He died on the eve of the twentieth anniversary, John and Michael at his bedside, relieving Terry Jones who had been with him shortly before. The planned celebrations were immediately dropped. 'The worst case of party-pooping I can remember,' said Terry.

At Graham's memorial service the Pythons each paid their tributes. Said John: 'We're all thinking how sad it is that a man of such talent, such capability and kindness, of such unusual intelligence should now be so suddenly spirited away at the age of only forty-eight, before he had

BELOW **The Pythons in a Bergmanesque moment as they ponder upon Death**

achieved many of the things of which he was capable, and before he had enough fun. Well, I feel I should say, "Nonsense. Good riddance to him, the free-loading bastard. I hope he fries." And the reason I think I should say this is that he would never forgive me if I didn't, if I threw away the opportunity to shock you all on his behalf. Anything for him but mindless good taste. I could hear him whispering in my ear last night as I was writing this, "All right, Cleese, you're very proud of being the first person to ever say 'shit' on television. If this service is really for me, just for starters, I want you to be the first person ever at a British memorial service to say "fuck".'

In the years since, the remaining Pythons have had to adjust to the reality that like all the great groups of their time – the Beatles, The Who, the Beach Boys – they have a dead member, rendering the possibility of a full reunion in the earthly life out of the question. Eric Idle has a morbid theory that they will all eventually succumb in alphabetical order, and keeps a close watch on John Cleese's health. Nevertheless it is Idle who is now actively attempting to effect a coming-together on stage of the survivors, which while not happening in time for the twenty-fifth anniversary, could be a possibility for the twenty-sixth or better still, the twenty-seventh. The idea is Python Live at Las Vegas, a show in that glittering desert nirvana that has now become the focal entertainment spot in the western hemisphere. 'Vegas is marvellous, now,' says Eric, 'Wonderful place for everyone, particularly if you find gambling boring, like me. The acts they have there are sensational,

and it doesn't matter how old you are. There's George Burns appearing at ninety-eight. He only started to be funny when he was in his eighties. The Pythons at Caesar's Palace would go down a treat. Even John thinks so, and he usually says no to everything. But for him and his blasted holiday we'd be doing it this Christmas.'

The Pythons are now comfortably removed from the present generation of comedians. Initially their influence was oppressive, and their immediate successors found themselves faced with an almost intolerable burden as they were first compared, and then found wanting. During the 1980s the grip began to be loosened as a new generation sprang out of *The Comic Strip* and elsewhere, Rik Mayall, Adrian Edmondson, French and Saunders, Lenny Henry and many others. But in the 1990s a deliberate anti-Python tendency was noticeable as stand-up comedians, working their audiences with minimal props and no funny costumes, became the vogue. The fact that they were reacting at all was a tribute to the ongoing influence of *Python* on British comedy. Pythonesque is a word that can be found in the more recent dictionaries, it defines a certain surreal approach to life. The group went through its cultish period, when intellectual writers attempted to correlate their work with Hegel, Brecht, Rabelais and Ernest Hemingway, to say nothing of Geoffrey Chaucer from the fourteenth century who probably did have an influence on their humour. The Pythons are now beyond such pseudery, although they have had to face a season at the National Film Theatre of their peripheral work, such as the two shows that were made in German.

The detractors will continue to carp, firstly because there have always been many people who could never stomach them, finding the use of humour as a conscious instrument of offensiveness an intolerable assault on their sensibilities, and secondly because there is an inevitable syndrome that nothing is ever as good as it was cracked up to be. One is reminded of Peter Sellers' old stage-doorkeeper recalling the golden era of British music-hall, who would say something like 'Dan Leno, Marie Lloyd, Harry Lauder, Vesta Tilley, Albert Chevalier – I knew 'em all and ... they were *terrible*!'

It is not a fate that should befall the the Pythons, though. Not yet anyway. For most of us, they were, and mostly still are, sheer bloody genius. And British.

LEFT **A dramatic end awaits the jumper in** ***The Meaning of Life***

THE END OF THE FILM

RIGHT **In true homage to the early days of television, Palin brings the viewers' attention to the end of** ***The Meaning of Life***

PYTHONOGRAPHY
Compiled by Lucy Douch

 TELEVISION

THAT WAS THE WEEK THAT WAS (BBC-1)
1st Series: 24 November 1962 to 27 April 1963
2nd Series: 28 September 1963 to 21 December 1963

THAT WAS THE WEEK THAT WAS
29 December 1962 and 28 December 1963
Produced and directed by Ned Sherrin.
Regular Cast: Davis Kernan, Roy Kinnear, William Rushton, Kenneth Cope, Lance Percival, Millicent Martin, with David Frost as linkman. Written contributions from **John Cleese**.

NOW (TWW)
1966
Teenage pop programme presented by **Michael Palin**.

FROST REPORT (BBC-1)
1st Series: 10 March 1966 to 28 April 1966
(1) on Authority (2) on Holidays (3) on Sin (4) on Elections (5) on Class (6) on The News (7) on Education (8) on Love
2nd Series: 6 April 1967 to 18 May 1967
(1) on Money (2) on Women (3) on The Forces (4) on untitled (5) on Parliament (6) on The Countryside (7) on Industry
Frost over Christmas 26 December 1967
Starring David Frost, with Ronnie Barker, Ronnie Corbett, **John Cleese**, Sheila Steafel, Julie Felix.
Written contributions from **John Cleese** (material sometimes co-written with **Graham Chapman**), **Michael Palin**, **Terry Jones**, and **Eric Idle**.
Prod James Gilbert.

ISADORA: THE BIGGEST DANCER IN THE WORLD (BBC-1)
22 September 1966
Starring Vivian Pickles.
Produced and directed by Ken Russell.
Uncredited appearances by **Michael Palin** and **Eric Idle** as members of a jazz band playing on the roof of a hearse.

THE LATE SHOW (BBC-1)
15 October 1966 to 17 December 1966, and 5 January 1967 to 1 April 1967
Prod Hugh Burnett (Jack Gold from 14 January 1967).
Michael Palin and **Terry Jones** wrote material and appeared.

THE FROST PROGRAMME (Rediffusion Network)
19 October 1966 to 4 January 1967
Presented by David Frost.
Prog Eds **John Cleese**, Tim Brooke-Taylor, Bryan Fitzjones, Michael Gowers, Peter Baker *Dir* Ian Fordyce
Prod Geoffrey Hughes.

ALICE IN WONDERLAND (BBC-1)
28 December 1966
Directed and produced by Jonathan Miller.
With Alan Bennett, John Bird, Wilfrid Brambell, Peter Cook, Sir John Gielgud, Malcolm Muggeridge, Sir Michael Redgrave, Peter Sellers and brief, uncredited appearance by **Eric Idle**.

AT LAST THE 1948 SHOW (Rediffusion)
1st Series: 15 February 1967 to 22 March 1967
2nd Series: 26 September 1967 to 7 November 1967
Written and performed by Tim Brooke-Taylor, **John Cleese**, **Graham Chapman**, Marty Feldman, with Aimi Macdonald.
Exec Prod David Frost *Dir* Ian Fordyce *Prod Eds* **John Cleese** and Tim Brooke-Taylor.

FROST OVER ENGLAND (BBC-1)
26 March 1967
Compilation of Frost Reports for BBC's entry for the Montreux Festival 1967, including sketches with **John Cleese**.
Additional material by **John Cleese** and **Graham Chapman**.

A SERIES OF BIRD'S (BBC-1)
3 October 1967 to 21 November 1967
Written by John Bird and John Fortune.
Prod Dennis Main Wilson.
Additional material by **Michael Palin** and **Terry Jones**.

TWICE A FORTNIGHT (BBC-1)
21 October 1967 to 23 December 1967
With Bill Oddie, Jonathan Lynn, Graeme Garden and Dilys Watling,
    plus **Michael Palin** and **Terry Jones**.
Introduced by Ronald Fletcher *Prod/Dir* Tony Palmer.

NO, THAT'S ME OVER HERE (Rediffusion Network)
14 November 1967 to 19 December 1967
Starring Ronnie Corbett.
Written by Barry Cryer, **Graham Chapman** and **Eric Idle**.
Exec Prod David Frost *Prod* Bill Hitchcock and Marty Feldman.

DO NOT ADJUST YOUR SET
1st Series: (Rediffusion Network) 4 January 1968 to 28 March 1968
2nd Series: (Thames Television) 19 February 1969 to 14 May 1969
Do Not Adjust Your Stocking 26 December 1968
Starring Denise Coffey, **Eric Idle**, David Jason, **Terry Jones**,
    Michael Palin.
Written by **Eric Idle**, **Terry Jones** and **Michael Palin** with animations
    by **Terry Gilliam**.
Prod Humphrey Barclay (1st series) Ian Davidson (2nd series)
Dir Daphne Shadwell (1st series) Adrian Cooper (2nd series)

MARTY (BBC-2)
1st Series: 29 April 1968 to 3 June 1968
2nd Series: 9 December 1968 to 13 January 1969
Starring Marty Feldman.
Additional material by **John Cleese**, **Graham Chapman**, **Terry Jones**,
    and **Michael Palin** (1st series).
Written by **John Cleese** and **Graham Chapman**, **Terry Jones** and
    Michael Palin (2nd series).
Prod Dennis Main Wilson *Dir* Roger Race.

WE HAVE WAYS OF MAKING YOU LAUGH
(London Weekend Television) 23 August 1968 to 18 October 1968
Presented by Frank Muir
Terry Gilliam Resident cartoonist. Written material and appearances
    by **Eric Idle**.
 Prod Humphrey Barclay *Dir* Bill Turner.

BROADEN YOUR MIND (BBC-2)
28 October 1968 to 2 December 1968
Starring Tim Brooke-Taylor and Graeme Garden.
Additional material from **John Cleese**, **Graham Chapman**, **Eric Idle**,
    Terry Jones, and **Michael Palin**.
Guest appearances by **Terry Jones**, **Michael Palin** and
    Graham Chapman.

THE COMPLETE AND UTTER HISTORY OF BRITAIN
(London Weekend Television)
12 January 1969 to 16 February 1969
1. From the Dawn of History to the Normal Conquest
2. Richard the Lionheart to Robin the Hood
3. Edward the First to Richard the Last
4. Perkin Warbeck to Bloody Mary
5. The Great and Glorious Age of Elizabeth
6. James the McFirst to Oliver Cromwell
Starring **Michael Palin** and **Terry Jones** plus Wallace Eaton,
    Colin Gordon, Roddy Maude-Roxby, Melinda Maye and
    Diana Quick.
Dir Maurice Murphy *Prod* Humphrey Barclay.
    Written by **Michael Palin** and **Terry Jones**.

DOCTOR IN THE HOUSE (London Weekend Television)
12 July 1969
'Why do you want to be a doctor?' by **John Cleese** and
    Graham Chapman. Based on the *Doctor* books by Richard Gordon.
Starring Barry Evans *Dir* David Askey *Prod* Humphrey Barclay.

MONTY PYTHON'S FLYING CIRCUS (BBC-1)
1st Series: 5 October 1969 to 26 October 1969, and 23 November 1969
    to 11 January 1970
2nd Series: 15 September 1970 to 29 September 1970, and 20 October
    1970 to 22 December 1970
3rd Series: 19 October 1972 to 21 December 1972, and 4 January 1973
    to 18 January 1973
Conceived, written and performed by **Graham Chapman**, **John Cleese**,
    Terry Gilliam, **Eric Idle**, **Terry Jones**, and **Michael Palin**.
Dir Ian McNaughton *Prod* John Howard Davies.
Animations by **Terry Gilliam**.
4th Series: **Monty Python** (BBC-2) 31 October 1974 to 5 December
    1974
Conceived, written and performed by **Graham Chapman**, **Terry
    Gilliam**, **Eric Idle**, **Terry Jones** and **Michael Palin**.
Additional material by **John Cleese**.
Dir Ian McNaughton *Prod* John Howard Davies.

LATE NIGHT LINE-UP (BBC-2)
12 January 1970
Presented by Joan Bakewell, Michael Dean, Tony Bilbow and
    Sheridan Morley.
Ed Rowan Ayers *Prod* Mike Fentiman.
Guests: **John Cleese**, **Graham Chapman**, **Terry Gilliam**, **Eric Idle** and
    Carol Cleveland.

THE MARTY FELDMAN COMEDY MACHINE (ATV)
8 October 1971 to 14 January 1972
Dir John Robins *Prod* Larry Gilbert *Exec Prod* Colin Clews.
Animations by **Terry Gilliam**.

183

COMEDY PLAYHOUSE (BBC-1)
14 January 1972
'Idle at Work' by **Graham Chapman** and Bernard McKenna.
Starring Ronnie Barker.
Prod James Gilbert *Dir* Harold Snoad.

ELEMENTARY, MY DEAR WATSON (BBC-1)
Comedy Playhouse 18 January 1973
Written by N. F. Simpson
Starring **John Cleese** as Sherlock Holmes and William Rushton as
    Dr Watson.
Prod Barry Took *Dir* Harold Snoad.

DOCTOR AT LARGE/IN CHARGE (London Weekend Television)
Varous episodes throughout 1972 and 1973 written by **John Cleese** and
    co-written (with Bernard McKenna/David Sherlock) by
    Graham Chapman.
Of special interest: 'No Ill Feelings' by **John Cleese**, 3 February 1973,
    featuring Timothy Bateson as Basil Fawlty prototype.
Dir Alan Wallis *Exec Prod* Humphrey Barclay.

SECRETS (BBC-2)
Black and Blue drama series, 14 August 1973
Written by **Michael Palin** and **Terry Jones**.
Starring Warren Mitchell.
Dir James Cellan Jones *Prod* Mark Shivas.

MONTY PYTHONS FIEGENDE ZIRKUS (BBC-2)
6 October 1973
Special German edition 'Schnapps with Everything'
Prod Thomas Woitkewitsch of Bavarian Atelier GmbH Munich for
    WDR.

LAUGHTER – WHY WE LAUGH (BBC-1)
14 October 1973
Written and presented by Barry Took, with **John Cleese**, Les Dawson
    and Peter Black.
Prod Vernon Lawrence.

THE DO-IT-YOURSELF FILM ANIMATION SHOW (BBC-1)
5 May 1974
Programme 3: 'Table top and cut-out animation'
Guest **Terry Gilliam**.
Presented by Bob Godfrey *Dir* Anna Jackson *Prod* David Hargreaves.

IN VISION (BBC-2)
6 December 1974
William Hardcastle meets Monty Python: a look back over five years of
    Monty Python's Flying Circus with extracts from some of the best
    and worst moments.
With **Graham Chapman**, **Terry Gilliam**, **Terry Jones** and
    Michael Palin.
Prod Peter Foges *Ed* Will Wyatt.

RUTLAND WEEKEND TELEVISION (BBC-2)
1st Series: 12 May 1975 to 16 June 1975
'Christmas with Rutland Weekend Television' 26 December 1975
2nd Series: 12 November 1976 to 24 December 1976
Written by **Eric Idle** *Dir* Andrew Gosling *Prod* Ian Keill.
Featuring **Eric Idle**, Neil Innes.

FAWLTY TOWERS (BBC-2)
1st Series: 19 September 1975 to 24 October 1975
2nd Series: 19 February 1979 to 18 March 1979, and 25 October 1979
Written by **John Cleese** and Connie Booth.
Starring **John Cleese**, Prunella Scales, Andrew Sachs and
    Connie Booth.
Prod John Howard Davies (1st series), Douglas Argent (2nd series).

THE SELLING LINE (BBC-2) Video Arts Ltd
6 October 1975 to 24 November 1975
Series written by **John Cleese** and Tony Jay
Featuring **John Cleese**
1. Who Sold You This, Then?
2. It's Alright, It's Only a Customer
3. The Competitive Spirit
4. In Two Minds
5. Awkward Customers
6. More Awkward Customers
7. I'll Think About It
8. How Not To Exhibit Yourself

THREE MEN IN A BOAT (BBC-2)
31 December 1975
Screenplay by Tom Stoppard.
Starring **Michael Palin**, Tim Curry and Stephen Moore.
Prod Rosemary Hill *Dir* Stephen Frears.

TOMKINSON'S SCHOOLDAYS (BBC-2)
7 January 1976
Written by **Michael Palin** and **Terry Jones**.
Produced and directed by Terry Hughes.
Starring **Michael Palin**, with **Terry Jones**.

OUT OF THE TREES (BBC-2)
10 January 1976
Featuring **Graham Chapman**.
Written by **Graham Chapman**, Bernard McKenna, Douglas Adams.
Prod Bernard Thompson.

FESTIVAL 40 (BBC-1)
16 August 1976
Monty Python's Flying Circus – special edition conceived, written and
    performed by **Graham Chapman**, **John Cleese**, **Terry Gilliam**,
    Eric Idle, **Terry Jones** and **Michael Palin**.
Prod Ian McNaughton.
Graham Chapman remembers Monty Python, interviewed by
    David Gillard.

PUNCH REVIEW (BBC-2)

4 January to 15 February 1977

Starring Robin Bailey, Julian Holloway.

Including material by **Michael Palin** and **Terry Jones**.

Prod Roger Race.

THREE PIECE SUITE (BBC-2)

12 April 1977

'Every Day in Every Way' by Alan Coren.

Starring Diana Rigg, **John Cleese**.

Prod Michael Mills.

THE STRANGE CASE OF THE END OF CIVILISATION AS WE KNOW IT (London Weekend Television)

18 September 1977

Written by Jack Hobbs, Joseph McGraph and **John Cleese**.

Starring **John Cleese** as A. Sherlock-Holmes, Arther Lowe and Connie Booth.

Dir Joseph McGrath *Prod* Humphrey Barclay.

RIPPING YARNS (BBC-2)

1st Series: 20 September 1977 to 25 October 1977

1. Tomkinson's Schooldays (*dir* Terry Hughes)
2. The Testing of Eric Holthwaite (*dir* Jim Franklin)
3. Escape from Stalag Luft 112B (*dir* Terry Hughes)
4. Murder at Moorstones Manor (*dir* Terry Hughes)
5. Across the Andes by Frog (*dir* Terry Hughes)
6. The Curse of the Claw (*dir* Jim Franklin)

2nd Series: 10 October 1979 to 24 October 1979

1. Whinfrey's Last Stand (*dir* Alan J W Bell)
2. Golden Gordon (*dir* Alan J W Bell)
3. Roger of Ray (*dir* Alan J W Bell)

Written by **Michael Palin** and **Terry Jones**.

THE MUPPET SHOW (ATV)

21 October 1977

Guest **John Cleese**.

Dir Philip Casson *Prod* Jim Henson.

THE RUTLES (BBC-2)

27 March 1978

Conceived and written by **Eric Idle**.

Music and lyrics by Neil Innes. Dir Gary Weis and **Eric Idle**.

Featuring **Eric Idle**, **Michael Palin**, Neil Innes, Mick Jagger, Ron Wood, Dan Ackroyd, Bill Murray, John Belushi.

THE PYTHONS (BBC-1)

20 June 1979

Documentary to commemorate the 10th anniversary of the 'best known British comedy group in the world'.

Prod/narrated by Iain Johnstone.

FRIDAY NIGHT, SATURDAY MORNING (BBC-2)

9 November 1979

Presented by Tim Rice.

Discussion between **John Cleese**, Michael Palin, Malcolm Muggeridge and Dr Mervyn Stockwood about *The Life of Brian*.

Dir John Burrowes *Prod* Iain Johnstone.

PETER COOK & CO (ITV)

14 September 1980

Starring Peter Cook, Rowan Atkinson, **John Cleese**, **Terry Jones**, Beryl Reid.

Dir/Prod Paul Smith.

THE TAMING OF THE SHREW (BBC-2)

23 October 1980

'BBC Television Shakespeare' series

Produced and directed by Jonathan Miller.

Starring **John Cleese** and Sarah Badel.

CONFESSIONS OF A TRAIN-SPOTTER (BBC-2)

27 November 1980

4th in a series of seven 'Great Railway Journeys of the World'.

Written by and featuring **Michael Palin**.

Prod Ken Stephinson *Series Prod* Roger Laughton.

DOCTOR WHO (BBC-1)

'The City of Death' final episode

1980/1981

Starring Tom Baker, Lalla Ward, Julian Glover.

Guest appearances by **John Cleese** and Eleanor Bron.

Written by Douglas Adams.

PAPERBACKS (BBC-1)

3 June 1981 to 15 July 1981

Introduced by **Terry Jones**.

Dir Nick Brenton *Prod* Rosemary Bowen-Jones, Julian Jebb.

THE INNES BOOK OF RECORDS (BBC-2)

28 September 1981

Starring Neil Innes.

Special guest **Michael Palin**.

Prod Ian Keill.

FRIDAY NIGHT...SATURDAY MORNING (BBC-2)

6 November 1981

Hosted by **Terry Jones**.

Prod Frances Whitaker.

WHOOPS APOCALYPSE (London Weekend Television)

Series of six beginning in December 1981

Starring Barry Morse, John Barron, Richard Griffiths, Alexei Sayle, Geoffrey Palmer, **John Cleese**.

Dir John Reardon *Prod* Humphrey Barclay.

THE RUPERT BEAR STORY (Channel Four)
A Tribute to Alfred Bestall
9 December 1982
Dir **Terry Jones** *Prod* Elizabeth Taylor-Mead.

GOOD MORNING, BRITAIN (TV-am)
1 February 1983
With **John Cleese** in his pyjamas.

STRICTLY PRIVATE (ITV)
3 March 1983
Programme about the making of *Privates on Parade* with **John Cleese**,
    Denis Quilley, Iain Johnstone.

COMIC ROOTS (BBC-2)
1983
Written by and starring **Michael Palin**.

THE YOUNG ONES (BBC-2)
29 May 1984
Guest appearance of **Terry Jones** as a drunk vicar.

OPINIONS (Channel 4)
1984
Written and presented by **Graham Chapman**.

CHEERS (Channel 4)
'Simon Says' 1987
Starring Ted Danson, Shelley Long, Rhea Perlman,
    Woody Harrelson. Guest starring **John Cleese**.
Prod David Angel *Dir* James Burrows.

STILL CRAZY LIKE A FOX (TV movie)
1986
Starring Jack Warden, John Rubinstein, Penny Peyser, Robby Kiger,
    Graham Chapman, Catherine Oxenberg.
Dir Paul Krasny

EAST OF IPSWICH (BBC-2)
1 February 1987
Starring Edward Rawle-Hicks, John Nettleton, Pat Heywood,
    Dona Kirsch.
Screenplay by **Michael Palin** *Dir* Tristram Powell.

THE MIKADO (Thames)
1987
Starring **Eric Idle** as Ko-Ko.
Dir Jonathan Miller *TV Dir* John Michael Phillips.

THE GRAND KNOCKOUT TOURNAMENT (BBC-1)
19 June 1987
Benefit led by Prince Edward, Princess Anne and the
Duke and Duchess of York.
Featuring **John Cleese** and **Michael Palin**.

AROUND THE WORLD IN 80 DAYS (BSB)
1988
Starring Pierce Brosnan as Fogg and **Eric Idle** as Passepartout.

THE CHAIRMAN (Central)
1988
Written by and starring **Michael Palin**.

NUMBER 27 (BBC-1)
23 October 1988
Starring Nigel Planer, Joyce Carey, Helena Michel, Alun Armstrong.
Screenplay by **Michael Palin** *Dir* Tristram Powell.

JOHN CLEESE'S FIRST FAREWELL PERFORMANCE (BBC-1)
A documentary on the making of *A Fish Called Wanda*.

ART OF TRAVEL (BBC North-East)
1989
Presented by **Michael Palin**.

AROUND THE WORLD IN 80 DAYS (BBC-1)
Series of six beginning on 11 October 1989
Written and presented by **Michael Palin**.
Dir Roger Mills and Clem Vallance.

SECRET POLICEMAN'S BIGGEST BALL (ITV)
October 1989
Starring **John Cleese**, **Michael Palin**, Peter Cook, Dudley Moore,
    Eleanor Bron, Robbie Coltrane, Ben Elton, Dawn French,
    Jeff Beck, Stephen Fry, Hugh Laurie, Mel Smith, Griff Rhys Jones.
Dirs **John Cleese** and Jennifer Saunders.

NEARLY DEPARTED (BBC-1)
1989
Starring **Eric Idle**, who also sang the theme song.

GBH (Channel 4)
Series of seven beginning on 6 June 1991
Starring **Michael Palin**, Robert Lindsay, Julie Walters,
    Lindsay Duncan.
Written by Alan Bleasdale. *Dir* Robert Young.

TOP OF THE POPS (BBC-1)
October 1991
Appearance by **Eric Idle**.

PRESENTS FROM THE PAST (BBC-1)
1991
Programme on the making of *American Friends*, with **Michael Palin**.

THE ROYAL VARIETY SHOW (LWT)
November 1991
Appearance by **Eric Idle**.

SO THIS IS PROGRESS? (BBC-2)
6 December 1991
Written and presented by **Terry Jones**.

ONE FOOT IN THE GRAVE (BBC-1)
December 1991 – Christmas Special
Starring Richard Wilson, Annette Crosby, **Eric Idle**.
Theme song sung by **Eric Idle**.

THE YOUNG INDIANA JONES CHRONICLES
Filmed in summer 1991
One episode directed by **Terry Jones**.

POLE TO POLE (BBC-1)
Series of eight beginning on 21 October 1992
Written and presented by **Michael Palin**.
Dir Roger Mills and Clem Vallance *Prod* Clem Vallance.

A CLASS ACT (Meridian TV)
9 January 1993
Starring **Michael Palin** and Tracey Ullman.
Dir Les Blair.

PALIN'S COLUMN (Meridian TV)
January 1994
Written and presented by **Michael Palin**.
Dir Roger Mills.

GREAT RAILWAY JOURNEYS (BBC-2)
February 1994
'Derry to Kerry'
Written and presented by **Michael Palin**.
Dir Ken Stephinson.

THE CRUSADES (BBC)
Autumn 1994
Written and presented by **Terry Jones**.
Prod Alan Ereira.

FILMS

INTERLUDE (1967) *Dir* Kevin Billington
Starring Oscar Werner, Barbara Ferris, Virginia Maskell, with
    John Cleese as a television PR man.

ALBERT CARTER Q.O.S.O. (1968) Dormer Productions
Short film starring Roy Kinnear with **Eric Idle**.

THE BLISS OF MRS BLOSSOM (1968) *Dir* Joseph McGrath
Starring Shirley MacLaine, Richard Attenborough, James Booth, with
    John Cleese as a shopkeeper.

THE MAGIC CHRISTIAN (1969) Dir Joseph McGrath
Starring Peter Sellers and Ringo Starr, with **John Cleese** as a director of
    Sotheby's and **Graham Chapman** as an Oxford stroke.
Screenplay by **Graham Chapman**, **John Cleese**, Peter Sellers,
    Terry Southern and Joseph McGrath.

THE RISE AND RISE OF MICHAEL RIMMER (1969)
Dir Kevin Billington
Starring Vanessa Redgrave, Peter Cook, Denholm Elliott,
    Ronald Fraser, Arthur Lowe, **John Cleese**.
Screenplay by **Graham Chapman**, **John Cleese**, Peter Cook and
    Kevin Billington.

THE CRY OF THE BANSHEE (1970) *Dir* Gordon Hessler
Starring Vincent Price and Elisabeth Bergner, with an uncredited
    appearance by **Terry Gilliam**.

DOCTOR IN TROUBLE (1970) *Dir* Ralph Thomas
Starring Leslie Phillips, Harry Secombe, James Robertson Justice, with
    Graham Chapman as Roddy.

THE STATUE (1970) *Dir* Rod Amateau
Starring David Niven, Virna Lisi, Robert Vaughn, Ann Bell, with
    John Cleese as Harry, a renegade psychiatrist.

AND NOW FOR SOMETHING COMPLETELY DIFFERENT (1971)
Dir Ian McNaughton
Written by and featuring **John Cleese**, **Graham Chapman**, **Eric Idle**,
    Terry Jones, **Michael Palin**.
Animations by **Terry Gilliam**.

WHO'S THERE? (1971) *Dir* Mike Wooler
Instructional film about canvassing produced by the Labour Party.
Starring **John Cleese**, **Graham Chapman**, **Terry Jones**, **Michael Palin**
    and Carol Cleveland.

THE LOVE BAN/IT'S A 2′ 6″ ABOVE THE GROUND WORLD
    (1972)
Dir Ralph Thomas
Starring Hywel Bennett, Nanette Newman, Milo O'Shea, **John Cleese**.

MONTY PYTHON AND THE HOLY GRAIL (1974) *Dir* **Terry Jones**
    and **Terry Gilliam**
Written by and featuring **John Cleese**, **Graham Chapman**, **Eric Idle**,
    Terry Jones, **Michael Palin**.
Animations by **Terry Gilliam**.

ROMANCE WITH A DOUBLE BASS (1974) *Dir* Robert Young
Starring **John Cleese** and Connie Booth.
Screen adaptation from Chekhov by **John Cleese** with Connie Booth
    and Robert Young.

THE MIRACLE OF FLIGHT (1974) *Dir* **Terry Gilliam**
Short animation.

PLEASURE AT HER MAJESTY'S (1976) *Dir* Roger Graef
With Alan Bennett, John Bird, Eleanor Bron, Tim Brooke-Taylor,
    John Cleese, Peter Cook, Bill Oddie, John Fortune, **Michael Palin**,
    Terry Jones.

JABBERWOCKY (1977) *Dir* **Terry Gilliam**
Starring **Michael Palin** as Dennis Cooper, Max Wall, John le Mesurier, Warren Mitchell and Harry H Corbett, with **Terry Jones** as a poacher.

THE ODD JOB (1978) *Dir* Peter Medak
Starring **Graham Chapman** as Arthur Harris, David Jason, Diana Quick.
Written and co-produced by **Graham Chapman**.

MONTY PYTHON'S LIFE OF BRIAN (1979) *Dir* **Terry Jones**
Written by and featuring **John Cleese**, **Graham Chapman**, **Eric Idle**, **Terry Jones** and **Michael Palin** with **Terry Gilliam**.

THE SECRET POLICEMAN'S BALL (1979) *Dir* Roger Graef
With Rowan Atkinson, Ken Campbell, **John Cleese**, Peter Cook, **Michael Palin**, Pete Townshend, John Williams, **Terry Jones**.
Stage direction by **John Cleese**.

AWAY FROM IT ALL (1979) *Dir* Clare Taylor, **John Cleese**
Narrated by Nigel Farquar-Bennet (**John Cleese**).

THE GREAT MUPPET CAPER (1981) *Dir* Jim Henson
Starring Charles Grodin, Diana Rigg with **John Cleese**.

TIME BANDITS (1981) *Dir* Terry Gilliam
Starring Sean Connery, Shelley Duvall, Ian Holm, **John Cleese**, David Warner, Craig Warnock.
Screenplay by **Terry Gilliam** and **Michael Palin**.

THE SECRET POLICEMAN'S OTHER BALL (1982)
Dir Julien Temple
With Rowan Atkinson, Alan Bennett, **Graham Chapman**, **John Cleese**, Billy Connolly, John Fortune, Alexei Sayle, Pamela Stephenson, John Wells.
Guest appearance by **Michael Palin**.

THE MISSIONARY (1982) *Dir* Richard Loncraine
Exec Prods George Harrison, Denis O'Brien
Co-prods **Michael Palin**, Neville C. Thompson
Starring **Michael Palin**, Maggie Smith, Trevor Howard, Michael Hordern.

MONTY PYTHON LIVE AT THE HOLLYWOOD BOWL (1982)
Dir Terry Hughes
Written and performed by **Graham Chapman**, **John Cleese**, **Terry Gilliam**, **Eric Idle**, **Terry Jones** and **Michael Palin**.
With Carol Cleveland, Neil Innes, Pamela Stephenson.

MONTY PYTHON'S MEANING OF LIFE (1983) *Dir* **Terry Jones**
Director of animation and special sequences: **Terry Gilliam**
Written and performed by **Graham Chapman**, **John Cleese**, **Terry Gilliam**, **Eric Idle**, **Terry Jones** and **Michael Palin**.

PRIVATES ON PARADE (1983) *Dir* Michael Blakemore
Starring **John Cleese**, Denis Quilley, Michael Elphick.

YELLOWBEARD (1983) *Dir* Mel Damski
Screenplay by **Graham Chapman**, Bernard McKenna, Peter Cook
Starring **Graham Chapman**, **John Cleese**, **Eric Idle**, Cheech and Chong, Madeline Kahn, Peter Cook, Marty Feldman.

A PRIVATE FUNCTION (1984) *Dir* Malcolm Mowbray
Starring **Michael Palin**, Maggie Smith, Denholm Elliott, Richard Griffiths, Bill Paterson, Liz Smith, Alison Steadman.

SILVERADO (1984) *Dir* Lawrence Kasdan
Starring Kevin Kline, Scott Glenn, Kevin Costner, Danny Glover, Brian Dennehy, Linda Hunt, Jeff Goldblum, Rosanna Arquette, **John Cleese**.

THE DRESS (1984) *Dir* Eva Sereny
Starring **Michael Palin**, Phyllis Logan, Derrick Branche, Dave Hill, Rachel Palin.

BRAZIL (1985) *Dir* **Terry Gilliam**
Screenplay by **Terry Gilliam**, Charles McKeown, Tom Stoppard.
Starring Jonathan Pryce, Robert De Niro, Katherine Helmond, Ian Holm, Bob Hoskins, **Michael Palin**, Ian Richardson.

CLOCKWISE (1985) *Dir* Christopher Morahan
Starring **John Cleese**, Alison Steadman, Sharon Maiden, Stephen Moore, Chip Sweeney, Penelope Wilton, Joan Hickson.

NATIONAL LAMPOON'S EUROPEAN VACATION (1985)
Dir Amy Heckerling
Starring Chevy Chase, Beverly D'Angelo, Dana Hill, Jason Lively, Victor Lanoux, John Astin, Paul Bartel, Mel Smith, **Eric Idle**.

SPIES LIKE US (1985) *Dir* John Landis
Starring Chevy Chase, Dan Ackroyd, Steve Forrest, Donna Dixon, Bruce Davison, Bernie Casey and Frank Oz, with a cameo appearance by **Terry Gilliam**.

LABYRINTH (1986) *Dir* Jim Henson
Screenplay by **Terry Jones**.
Starring David Bowie, Jennfier Connelly, Toby Froud, Shelley Thompson, Christopher Malcolm, Natalie Webster.

THE TRANSFORMERS – THE MOVIE (1986) *Dir* Nelson Shin
Cartoon featuring the voices of **Eric Idle**, Judd Nelson, Leonard Nimoy, Robert Stack, Lionel Stander, Orson Welles.

PERSONAL SERVICES (1987) *Dir* **Terry Jones**
Starring Julie Walters, Alec McCowen, Danny Schiller, Shirley Stelfox, Victoria Hardcastle, Tim Woodward, Dave Atkins.

THE SECRET POLICEMAN'S THIRD BALL (1987) *Dir* Ken O'Neill
Starring Joan Armatrading, **John Cleese**, Robbie Coltrane, Phil Cool, Duran Duran, Stephen Fry, Hugh Laurie, Ben Elton.

A FISH CALLED WANDA (1988)
Screenplay by **John Cleese**
Dir Charles Crichton and **John Cleese**
Starring **John Cleese**, Jamie Lee Curtis, Kevin Kline, **Michael Palin**,
   Maria Aitken, Tom Georgeson, Patricia Hayes, Geoffrey Palmer.

THE ADVENTURES OF BARON MUNCHAUSEN (1989)
Screenplay by **Terry Gilliam**, Charles McKeown
Dir **Terry Gilliam**
Starring John Neville, Sarah Polley, **Eric Idle**, Charles McKeown,
   Winston Dennis, Jack Purvis, Valentina Cortese, Uma Thurman,
   Oliver Reed, Jonathan Pryce, Bill Paterson, Robin Williams, Sting.

ERIK THE VIKING (1989) *Dir Terry Jones*
Screenplay by **Terry Jones**
Starring Tim Robbins, Mickey Rooney, Eartha Kitt, **Terry Jones**,
   Imogen Stubbs, **John Cleese**, Tsutomu Sekine, Antony Sher,
   Gary Cady, Charles McKeown, Tim McInnerny,
   John Gordon Sinclair, Freddie Jones.

THE BIG PICTURE (1989) *Dir* Christopher Guest
Starring Kevin Bacon, Emily Longstreth, JT Walsh, with a cameo
   appearance by **John Cleese**.

NUNS ON THE RUN (1990) *Dir* Jonathan Lynn
Starring **Eric Idle**, Robbie Coltrane, Camille Coduri, Janet Suzman,
   Doris Hare, Lila Kaye, Robert Patterson.

TOO MUCH SUN (1990) *Dir* Robert Downey Sr.
Starring **Eric Idle**, Andrea Martin, Alan Arkin, Robert Downey Jr.

AMERICAN FRIENDS (1991) *Dir* Tristram Powell
Screenplay by **Michael Palin** & Tristram Powell. Starring **Michael
   Palin**, Trini Alvarado, Connie Booth, Bryan Pringle, Fred Pearson,
   Alfred Molina, Robert Eddison, Alun Armstrong.

AN AMERICAN TAIL: FIEVEL GOES WEST (1991)
Dir Phil Nibbelink and Simon Wells
Cartoon featuring the voices of Phillip Glasser, James Stewart,
   Nehemiah Persoff, Amy Irving, **John Cleese**, Dom DeLuise.

MISSING PIECES (1991)
Starring **Eric Idle**.

THE FISHER KING (1991) *Dir* Terry Gilliam
Starring Robin Williams, Jeff Bridges, Amanda Plummer,
   Mercedes Ruehl, Michael Jeter, Harry Shearer.

MOM AND DAD SAVE THE WORLD (1992) *Dir* Greg Beeman
Starring Teri Garr, Jeffrey Jones, Jon Lovitz, Wallace Shawn, **Eric Idle**.

SPLITTING HEIRS (1993) *Dir* Robert Young
Screenplay by **Eric Idle**.
Starring **Eric Idle**, Rick Moranis, Barbara Hershey,
   Catherine Zeta Jones, **John Cleese**, Sadie Frost, Stratford Johns,
   Brenda Bruce, Eric Sykes.

MONTY PYTHON'S BIG RED BOOK 1971

THE BRAND NEW MONTY PYTHON BOOK Methuen 1973
   (issued in paperback as *The Brand New Monty Python
   Papperbok*/Methuen 1974)

MONTY PYTHON AND THE HOLY GRAIL (BOOK)
Edited by **Terry Jones**/Designed by Derek Birdsall/Methuen 1977

MONTY PYTHON'S LIFE OF BRIAN
Edited by **Eric Idle**/ Designed by Basil Pao/Methuen 1979

**THE COMPLETE WORKS OF SHAKESPEARE AND MONTY
   PYTHON: VOLUME ONE – MONTY PYTHON**
Methuen 1981 (combined re-issue of *Monty Python's Big Red Book* and
   The Brand New Monty Python Book)

BERT FEGG'S NASTY BOOK FOR BOYS AND GIRLS
Terry Jones and **Michael Palin**/Methuen 1974

RUTLAND DIRTY WEEKEND BOOK
Eric Idle/Methuen 1976

HELLO SAILOR
Eric Idle/Futura 1976

SPORTING RELATIONS
Roger McGough/Illustrated by **Terry Gilliam**/Methuen 1976

**THE STRANGE CASE OF THE END OF CIVILISATION AS WE
   KNOW IT**
John Cleese and Jack Hobbs/Star Books 1977

FAWLTY TOWERS
John Cleese and Connie Booth/Contact Publications 1977

ANIMATIONS OF MORTALITY
Terry Gilliam/Methuen 1978

RIPPING YARNS
Terry Jones and **Michael Palin**/Methuen 1978

FAWLTY TOWERS BOOK 2
John Cleese and Connie Booth/Weidenfeld and Nicholson 1979

**MONTY PYTHON SCRAPBOOK OF BRIAN OF NAZARETH/
   THE LIFE OF BRIAN**
Methuen 1979

MORE RIPPING YARNS
Michael Palin/Methuen 1980

A LIAR'S AUTOBIOGRAPHY
Graham Chapman/Methuen 1980

**CHAUCER'S KNIGHT – THE PORTRAIT OF A MEDIEVAL
   MERCENARY**
Terry Jones/Weidenfeld and Nicholson 1980

FAIRY TALES
Terry Jones/Illustrated by Michael Foreman/Pavilion Books 1981

GREAT RAILWAY JOURNEYS OF THE WORLD
Michael Frayn, Ludovic Kennedy, Miles Kington, **Michael Palin**, Eric Robson, Brian Thompson, Michael Wood/BBC 1981

TIME BANDITS: A SCREENPLAY
Michael Palin and **Terry Gilliam**/Hutchinson 1981

THE MISSIONARY
Michael Palin/Methuen 1982

PASS THE BUTLER
Eric Idle/Methuen 1982

SMALL HARRY AND THE TOOTHACHE PILLS
Michael Palin/Illustrated by Caroline Holden/Methuen 1982

MONTY PYTHON'S THE MEANING OF LIFE
Methuen 1983

FAMILIES AND HOW TO SURVIVE THEM
John Cleese and **Robin Skynner**/Methuen 1983

THE SAGA OF ERIK THE VIKING
Terry Jones/Illustrated by Michael Foreman/Pavilion Books 1983

DR FEGG'S ENCYCLOPAEDIA (SIC) OF ALL WORLD KNOWLEDGE
Terry Jones and **Michael Palin**/Methuen 1984

THE GOLDEN SKITS OF WING COMMANDER MURIEL VOLESTRANGLER FRHS AND BAR
John Cleese/Methuen 1984

LIMERICKS
Michael Palin/Illustrated by Tony Ross/Century Hutchinson 1985

NICOBOBINUS
Terry Jones/Illustrated by Michael Foreman/Pavilion Books 1985

CYRIL AND THE DINNER PARTY
Michael Palin/Illustrated by Caroline Holden/Pavilion Books 1986

CYRIL AND THE HOUSE OF COMMONS
Michael Palin/Illustrated by Caroline Holden/Pavilion Books 1986

THE MIRRORSTONE
Michael Palin, Alan Lee, Richard Seymour/Jonathan Cape 1986

GOBLINS OF THE LABYRINTH
Terry Jones/Illustrated by Brian Froud/Pavilion Books 1986

THE MONTY PYTHON GIFT BOKS
Comprising of *Monty Python's Big Red Book* and *The Brand New Monty Python Papperbok*/Methuen 1986

A FISH CALLED WANDA
John Cleese and Charles Crichton/Methuen 1988

ATTACKS OF OPINION
Terry Jones/Illustrated by Gerald Scarfe/Penguin 1988

THE COMPLETE FAWLTY TOWERS
John Cleese and Connie Booth/Methuen 1988

THE CURSE OF THE VAMPIRE'S SOCKS AND OTHER DOGGEREL
Terry Jones/Illustrated by Michael Foreman/Pavilion Books 1988

AROUND THE WORLD IN 80 DAYS
Michael Palin/BBC Books 1989

ERIK THE VIKING
Terry Jones/Methuen 1989

ERIK THE VIKING (COMIC STRIP)
Terry Jones/Illustrated by Graham Thompson/Robson Books 1989

MONTY PYTHON'S FLYING CIRCUS – JUST THE WORDS
Methuen 1989

THE ADVENTURES OF BARON MUNCHAUSEN
Charles McKeown and **Terry Gilliam**/Methuen 1989

THE COMPLETE RIPPING YARNS
Terry Jones and **Michael Palin**/Methuen 1990

FANTASTIC STORIES
Terry Jones/Illustrated by Michael Foreman/Pavilion Books 1992

POLE TO POLE
Michael Palin/BBC 1992

A FISH OF THE WORLD
Terry Jones/Illustrated by Michael Foreman/Pavilion Books 1993

THE BEAST WITH A THOUSAND TEETH
Terry Jones/Illustrated by Michael Foreman/Pavilion Books 1993

THE FLY-BY-NIGHT
Terry Jones/Illustrated by Michael Foreman/Pavilion Books 1993

THE SEA TIGER
Terry Jones/Illustrated by Michael Foreman/Pavilion Books 1993

LIFE AND HOW TO SURVIVE IT
John Cleese and Robin Skynner/Methuen 1993

LADY COTTINGTON'S PRESSED FAIRY BOOK
As discovered by **Terry Jones** and Brian Froud/Pavilion Books 1994

GREAT RAILWAY JOURNEYS
Clive Anderson, Natalia Makarova, Rian Malan, **Michael Palin**, Lisa St Aubin de Teràn, Mark Tully/BBC 1994

POLE TO POLE – THE PHOTOGRAPHS
Michael Palin/Photographs by Basil Pao/BBC 1994

THE CRUSADES
Terry Jones and Alan Ereira/BBC 1994

THE FAIRLY INCOMPLETE AND RATHER BADLY ILLUSTRATED MONTY PYTHON SONGBOOK
Methuen 1994

THE WEEKEND
Michael Palin/Methuen 1994

RECORDINGS

MONTY PYTHON'S FLYING CIRCUS
1970/BBC Records/REB 73M

ANOTHER MONTY PYTHON RECORD
1971/Charisma/CAS 1049

MONTY PYTHON'S PREVIOUS RECORD
1972/Charisma/CAS 1063

THE MONTY PYTHON MATCHING TIE AND HANDKERCHIEF
1973/Charisma/CAS 1080

MONTY PYTHON LIVE AT DRURY LANE
1974/Charisma/Class 4

THE ALBUM OF THE SOUNDTRACK OF THE TRAILER OF THE FILM OF MONTY PYTHON AND THE HOLY GRAIL
1975/Charisma/CAS 1103

THE RUTLAND WEEKEND SONGBOOK
1975/BBC Records/REB 233

A POKE IN THE EYE WITH A SHARP STICK
1976/Transatlantic/TRA 331
Recording of the 1976 Amnesty Show with **Graham Chapman**, **John Cleese**, **Terry Gilliam**, **Terry Jones**, **Michael Palin**, Carol Cleveland, Neil Innes, Alan Bennett, John Bird, Eleanor Bron, Tim Brooke-Taylor, Peter Cook

MONTY PYTHON LIVE AT CITY CENTER
1976/Kay Gee Bee Songs Inc/AB 4073
Recording of stage show at City Center, New York

MERMAID FROLICS
1977/Polydor/2384101
Recording of the 1977 Amnesty show with **John Cleese**, **Terry Jones**, Connie Booth, Julie Covington, Jonathan Miller, Peter Ustinov, The Bowles Brothers

THE MONTY PYTHON INSTANT RECORD COLLECTION
1977/Charisma/CAS 1134

THE RUTLES: ALL YOU NEED IS CASH
1978/Warner Bros/K 56459

FAWLTY TOWERS
1979/BBC Records/REB 377

THE SECRET POLICEMAN'S BALL
1979/Island/ILPS 9601

MONTY PYTHON'S LIFE OF BRIAN
1994/Virgin

MONTY PYTHON'S CONTRACTURAL OBLIGATION ALBUM
1980/Charisma/CAS 1152

FAWLTY TOWERS: SECOND SITTING
1981/BBC Records/REB 405

THE SECRET POLICEMAN'S OTHER BALL
1981/Island/HAHA 6003

FAWLTY TOWERS AT YOUR SERVICE
1982/BBC Records/REB 449

MONTY PYTHON'S THE MEANING OF LIFE
1994/Virgin

JACK THE GIANT KILLER/SCRAPEFOOT
1984/LP 204 (AC)

MOWGLI'S BROTHERS
1984/LP205 (AC)

HOW FEAR CAME
1984/LP 206 (AC)
Read by **Michael Palin**

ALADDIN AND THE WONDERFUL LAMP
1984/LP 214 (AC)

THE VOYAGES OF SINBAD (I TO III)
1984/LP 212 (AC)

THE VOYAGES OF SINBAD (IV TO VI)
1984/LP 213 (AC)
Read by **Terry Jones**

THE MIKADO
1986/MCA/MCAD-6215
Featuring Eric Idle as Ko-Ko

MONTY PYTHON SINGS
1989/Virgin/Mont 1

ALWAYS LOOK ON THE BRIGHT SIDE
1991/Virgin/Pyth 1
7-inch single

GALAXY SONG
1991/Virgin/Pyth2
7-inch single

FAMILES AND HOW TO SURVIVE THEM
Written and read by Robin Skynner and **John Cleese**/BBC Radio Collection 1991

BRAZIL – THE SOUNDTRACK
Milan 1992/11124-2 (CD)

THE MAN
1992/Random Century
Written by Raymond Briggs. Read by **Michael Palin**

AROUND THE WORLD IN 80 DAYS
1993/BBC Audio Collection
Written and read by **Michael Palin**

JACK AND THE BEANSTALK
1993/Rabbit Ears
Read by **Michael Palin**

ESIO TROT
1994/Random Century
Written by Roald Dahl. Read by **Michael Palin**

THE MONTY PYTHON INSTANT CD COLLECTION
(Box set featuring all *Python* original albums)
1994/Virgin

 PICTURE CREDITS

*The publisher has endeavoured to acknowledge all copyright holders of the
pictures reproduced in this book. However, should any photographs not be
correctly attributed, the publisher undertakes to make any appropriate changes
in future editions of the book*

Amnesty International

Humphrey Barclay Collection

BBC

BFI Stills, Posters and Design, London

Channel 4

John Cleese and Connie Booth

*Columbia/Tri-Star, Embassy, EMI, HandMade, MGM, Orion, Prominent,
Touchstone, Umbrella, Universal, Vestron, Warner*

Robert Hewison

National Film Archive

Newark Advertiser

Pavilion Books

Radio Times

Bill Rafferty

Thames TV

Time Out

John Cleese taken from Video Arts Programmes Decisions, Decisions
and The Control of Working Capital. Video Arts Ltd